How to Use
EVERNOTE
for Genealogy

How to Use EVERNOTE for Genealogy

a **STEP-BY-STEP GUIDE** to organize your research and boost your genealogy productivity

KERRY SCOTT

FAMILY TREE BOOKS

Cincinnati, Ohio
shopfamilytree.com

CONTENTS

CHAPTER 1
Evernote isn't quite like any other genealogy tool. In this chapter, we'll discuss just
what this free software is all about and why it's exactly what you need to become a
better genealogist.

CHAPTER 2
In this chapter, we'll go over how to download Evernote, set up an account, and cre-
ate your first note. We'll also discuss in detail the big question: Basic (free) account,
Plus subscription, or Premium subscription?

CHAPTER 3
Sometimes it's hard to get started because you're stuck on trying to figure out an
organization scheme. In this chapter, we'll explore a variety of ways to structure your
data. We'll also talk about Evernote's built-in tools to keep you organized.

CHAPTER 4
It's no use having lots of great information about your ancestors if you can't find it
again. Evernote has you covered with a fast, user-friendly search function. In this
chapter, we'll go over how to ensure you can find exactly what you need, when you
need it.

CHAPTER 5
Tags aren't just for finding what you're looking for. They're a secret weapon you
can use to help analyze your data and spot patterns, hidden clues, and connections
between people, places, and things. In this chapter, you'll find lots of ideas on how to
use tags to break down your brick walls.

CHAPTER 6
In this chapter, we'll explore all the genealogy items you can include in your Evernote notes. From photos to documents to web clippings to audio files, you'll learn
exactly how to work with the wide range of information Evernote can accommodate.

CHAPTER 7

SHARING AND COLLABORATING

Dead people are great, but most of us have to occasionally interact with living cousins and colleagues at some point. This chapter will show you all of the ways Evernote can make the collaboration process run smoothly so you can concentrate on finding more ancestors.

CHAPTER 8

PUTTING IT ALL TOGETHER

How does a real-life genealogist use Evernote on a daily basis? In this chapter, you'll find out. You'll see concrete examples and a long list of ideas for how you can use Evernote to be a more successful family historian.

CHAPTER 9

SYNCING AND SECURING YOUR EVERNOTE DATA ON MOBILE DEVICES

Evernote is portable, and it works on all of your devices. That's a great benefit, but it brings some special security challenges. In this chapter, we'll talk about how to keep your important data safe and secure, even on the road.

CHAPTER 10

ENHANCING EVERNOTE WITH EXTERNAL TOOLS

A host of add-ons make Evernote even better. In this chapter, we'll talk about tools to help you get the most out of your Evernote experience.

CHAPTER 11

PROTECTING YOUR EVERNOTE FILES

As genealogists, we know the importance of being good stewards of our family's history. This chapter will show you how to back up your data in a number of ways so they're preserved for future generations.

CHAPTER 12

TROUBLESHOOTING

Sometimes things go wrong. Before you panic, check out this chapter, where you'll find solutions for the most common stumbling blocks for Evernote users. We'll also talk about where to go for more help, advice, and support when you need it.

INTRODUCTION

The first time I tried Evernote, I hated it. I couldn't see the point at all. I opened it up, and it looked more or less like a word processor. I couldn't see what all the hype was about. I already knew how to use a word processor, and I couldn't imagine why anyone would use one just to take notes. That's what a pen and paper are for, right?

I closed the application and left it closed for more than a year.

When I heard another mom talking about how she used Evernote to manage her household, I decided to give it another try. I have a husband, two kids, a business, and a habit of going on multiday genealogy benders. Any tool that helps life run smoothly (and free up more time for genealogy) is one I want to check out.

I quickly learned that my initial assessment had been totally wrong. Evernote is actually the key to being a more efficient, more effective person in every part of my life. It's been especially helpful in making me a better genealogist. I'm able to get more done, spot clues and patterns more quickly, and ensure that I don't ever do the same research twice. It's the Swiss Army knife in my genealogy toolbox (and in my life management toolbox, for that matter). I couldn't live without it.

Learning to use Evernote was a bit of a lonely process for me. At the time I was getting started, not many other genealogists were using it. The books I found on the subject were mostly geared toward salespeople and other corporate types. There weren't really any educational resources available to show me how this program could be used for family history. In writing this book, I've aimed to create the guide I wished I had as I was learning to use Evernote.

Whether you're just getting started or you're already an Evernote ninja, I believe you'll find many helpful tips and tricks in this book. I've tried to share as many real-life genealogy examples as I can so you can see how Evernote can make you a better genealogist. I think you'll find, as I did, that this tool is the key to connecting with your family—living or dead.

Kerry Scott
<www.cluewagon.com>

Getting Acquainted
with Evernote

Sooner or later, it happens to every genealogist. No matter how organized you are, you'll inevitably find that the sheer volume of information you're gathering in pursuit of your ancestors brings you to your knees. Where did all of this stuff come from? How do you keep it organized? How do you make sense of it?

Evernote can help. It's no exaggeration to say that this tool can and will change your research life. Evernote gives you a place to organize all of your genealogical data, no matter what form. It also has a powerful search feature so you can actually find your data again. Evernote has tools to allow you to analyze what you've found in a variety of ways so you can see the hidden clues in even the most unlikely places. It's one of the best weapons available for breaking down those long-standing brick walls, for keeping you organized, and for freeing up more time to find your ancestors.

In this chapter, we'll explore what Evernote can do for you and why it's uniquely suited to meet the needs of genealogists looking for better ways to sift through their family history info as well as their hard-earned research.

TYPES OF RECORDS

One of Evernote's greatest strengths for genealogy is the breadth and depth of items it can track for you. We genealogists gather clues from a variety of sources, from census records to scraps of paper to the embroidery on Great-grandma Ethel's quilt. Evernote takes them all in stride. In this section, we'll explore some of the types of records you can keep in Evernote so you can make the most of what this software has to offer.

Text Notes

Most Evernote genealogists start out by taking notes (image 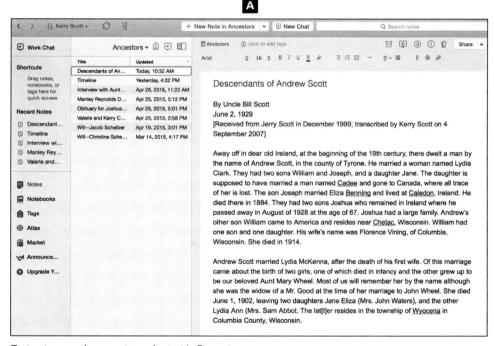). When you first open Evernote, you'll be greeted by a blank screen. Create a note (more on this in chapter 2), then start typing. You can use the note for anything you like—a transcription of a will, notes on a local genealogical society presentation, free-form thoughts on what you remember about Grandpa Joe, the citation for a source you found while researching, or whatever else you'd like to capture.

A

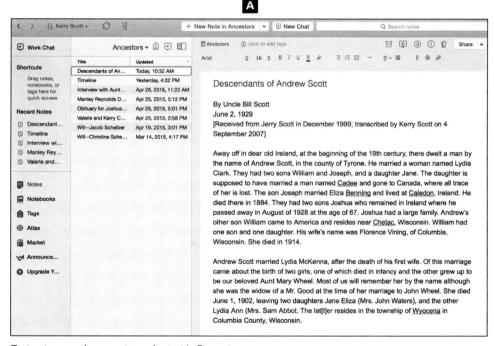

Text notes are where most people start in Evernote.

If you have old census abstracts from the days before the Internet, scan them into Evernote so you can find and use them easily.

Handwritten Notes

Still like taking notes the old-fashioned way? No problem. You can take notes on paper, then scan them into Evernote (or just take a photo using your smartphone or tablet). If you've used preprinted note-taking forms for genealogy (image **B**), this feature can come in handy. Depending on the quality of your printing, you might even be able to search your handwritten notes. If you have an iPad, an Android tablet, or a Windows tablet, you can use a stylus and a special app to write notes directly onto your tablet—no paper required.

Photos of People and Things

Most genealogists have at least a few treasured photos of ancestors. Some of us are lucky enough to have inherited heirlooms, such as china, jewelry, artwork, recipe cards, or other artifacts—or we might have pictures of the heirlooms in other relatives' possession. Nearly all of us have photos of cemetery headstones and homes or other buildings associated with our ancestors. All of these images belong in Evernote, where they can be cataloged, searched, tagged, and linked to tell the full story of our ancestors (images **C** and **D**).

The headstones of twelve of my ancestors appear in this photo. It's in my Evernote file, tagged with the names of each of those twelve people so I can find it when I'm working on one of those ancestors.

Photos of Documents

One of the most revolutionary uses of Evernote for genealogists is the capture of documents (image **E**). Once you know how to use Evernote's built-in camera feature on your smartphone or tablet, you'll never again need a flash drive or a photocopy card while doing on-site research. You won't need a scanner for routine document capture, either. That means you can photograph, tag, and save that marriage certificate the day it arrives in the mail. It won't sit in your meaning-to-scan pile for months (or years, if you're like me).

Audio Files

It's one of the first pieces of advice every new genealogist receives: "Interview your relatives." Back in the olden days, we might have frantically taken notes during that interview or recorded it on tape (remember tapes?). Nowadays, you can use Evernote's built-in recording feature to capture Aunt Ruby's own voice while you ask her about her grandparents (image **F**). Because most of us have a mobile device with us while visiting, we don't have to plan ahead, bring extra batteries, stock up on blank tapes, or any of that other rigmarole from a bygone era. Evernote makes it so much simpler.

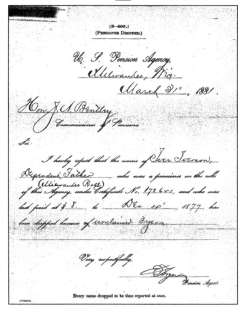

This clock sits on my family's mantel today, but it was originally a wedding gift to my great-grandparents in 1913. I have it tagged with my other documents and notes related to that wedding.

This important page from the Civil War pension file of Iver Iverson tells me when his pension went unclaimed, which led me to his death date. I have it in Evernote for safekeeping and easy access.

PDFs

Most genealogists collect an enormous number of PDFs over time. From conference syllabi to *Family Tree Magazine* articles to documents from cousins, this file format is everywhere. Fortunately, Evernote allows you to store and search PDFs (image **G**). If you decide to purchase an Evernote Premium account, you can even annotate PDFs with text, arrows, circles, highlighting, and more. You can also convert your Evernote notes to PDF files, making them easier to store, share, and back up.

POWER-USER TIP

Recording Family Interviews

Many apps allow you to record interviews with family members, and most of them record in an MP3 format. This is great for storing music, but because MP3 files are compressed, you lose some sound quality. Evernote's built-in recording app records your interviews in a WAV format, which creates an uncompressed file that is much better for capturing and preserving speech.

This audio file from 1990 is the only one we have that features the voice of my kids' great-grandfather. This old CD no longer plays properly, but fortunately, I saved the audio file to Evernote.

I subscribe to the digital version of *Family Tree Magazine* and store the PDFs in Evernote. When I find an article that will help my research, I tag it with that family's surname. That way, I'll find it even when I've forgotten about the article.

Web Clippings

It seems like every genealogist starts out on the Internet. Those Ancestry.com "shaky leaf" commercials lure them in, and the Internet keeps them clicking on link after link. As genealogists become more experienced, they tend to branch out into in-person research at libraries, archives, cemeteries, and so forth, but the Internet is still the most frequent stomping ground of most genealogists. So we all need a tool to manage our online research efforts. Evernote allows you to capture information in your web browser in seconds and automatically send it to your Evernote file (see image **H**). Even better, it captures the link where the information came from so you don't have to wonder where you got it. That makes building strong source citations much easier. It also saves you a lot of work when you realize you need more data than you thought from that original website.

To-Do Lists

Many of us occasionally resemble a dog on a walk to the park when we do research. We're focused on the walk—but wait. Let's sniff this tree. And this rock. And this bench. Is that a *squirrel*?

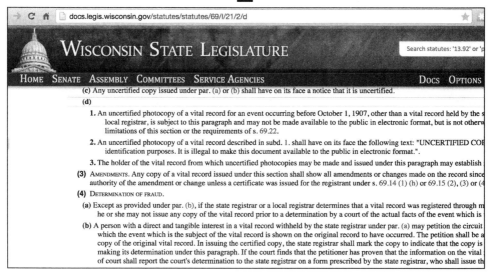

I took this screenshot of Wisconsin's unusually restrictive law regarding making copies of vital records. Thank goodness I still had it in my Evernote file, because it was helpful when deciding what records to use as examples for this book. Thanks to Evernote's robust search capabilities, it was easy to find when I needed it.

When we're hot on the trail of an ancestor, it's easy to get sidetracked and end up researching that ancestor's stepchild's mother's sister's second husband. To-do lists can help us stay focused by giving us a place to log those tempting side projects for follow-up. Evernote has a built-in to-do list feature (image **I**) that allows you to check tasks off as you complete them and to tag them to cross-reference with the notes they relate to.

Research and Correspondence Logs

Most of us know we should be keeping track of the sources we've already searched so we don't duplicate our efforts. But how many of us actually do it? Evernote makes it so easy to log our efforts that it's far more likely we'll actually take this important step. A research log documents what we've looked for, what the results were, and when we did the work (so we can come back to it as new resources become available). A correspondence log records what we've ordered online or via mail so we don't accidentally request (and pay for) the same record twice. Both of these features can save a great deal of time and money—and with Evernote, it's easy to search our research and correspondence logs to ensure we can find those critical details, even years after we've forgotten all about them (image **J**).

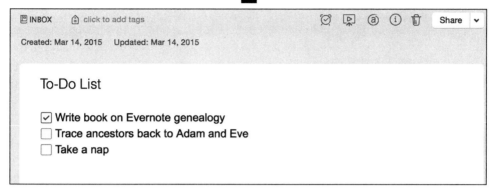

Keep track of all the side projects you want to get to "someday" by putting them on a to-do list like this one.

Shared via Work Chat				Share ⌄
Created: Mar 11, 2013 Updated: May 3, 2015				

You are editing a note that is shared with 1 person and discussed in 1 chat

SEN Tree (Severina Elizabeth Nelson)

Date	Call Number	Description of Source	Purpose of Search	Results
11 March 2013		FamilySearch.org, Minnesota, County Birth Records 1863-1983 > Freeborn, Bath > Births, Deaths 1872-1896, Vol. A	Births or deaths of anyone with Hans/Barbara Peterson, Sigrid/Nils Nelson, Engebrit/Golete Erickson, Anna & Erick Arneson, Gjiskan and Lauritz Nelson, Nels/Kristine Nelson, Nels/Alice Nelson or Betsy/Christ Klavberg as parents; death of Karen Iverson	See files; death of Karen Iverson not found
26 March 2013		FamilySearch.org, Minnesota, County Birth Records 1863-1983 > Freeborn, Bath > Births, Deaths 1896-1900, Vol. B	Births or deaths of anyone with Hans/Barbara Peterson, Sigrid/Nils Nelson, Engebrit/Golete Erickson, Anna & Erick Arneson, Gjiskan and Lauritz Nelson, Nels/Kristine Nelson, Nels/Alice Nelson or Betsy/Christ Klavberg as parents; death of Karen Iverson or Hans and Barbara Peterson	See files (one birth to Lauritz and Gjisken Nelson). Hans not found in Bath township (probably in Albert Lea or "east of town" where he died). Barbara not found.
26 March 2013		FamilySearch.org, Minnesota, County Birth Records 1863-1983 > Freeborn, Bath > Births, Deaths 1900-1907, Vol. C	Births or deaths of anyone with Hans/Barbara Peterson, Sigrid/Nils Nelson, Engebrit/Golete Erickson, Anna & Erick Arneson, Gjiskan and Lauritz Nelson, Nels/Kristine Nelson, Nels/Alice Nelson or Betsy/Christ Klavberg as parents; death of Karen Iverson or Barbara Peterson	See files--one death, Luella Josephine Nelson). Barbara not found.
26 March 2013		FamilySearch.org, Minnesota, County Birth Records 1863-1983 > Freeborn > Birth Index, 1870-1920, Vol. A	All Nelson/Nilson/Nielson children born to Nels and Sigrid or Nels and Kristine or Nels and Oline/Alice in appropriate respective timeframes (images 206 through 215; also looked through subsequent images to see if there were any from 1888-1894)	"Serine Elizabeth Nelsen" on 23 Sept 1882 th Nils and Kristine (name of child clearly written in later); Allert included (but no correction later--probably because no Social Security): NO

Evernote is ideal for research logs. You won't have to worry about which name to file the log under because all of the anestor names included will be equally searchable.

WHY EVERNOTE IS PERFECT FOR GENEALOGISTS

Although Evernote wasn't specifically designed for genealogists, the more you use it, the more you realize it's ideal for our community's unique needs. No other available tool is quite like it, and it can be adapted and expanded to work for both brand-new and experienced genealogists. Here are four key benefits of using Evernote.

It's Highly Searchable

Even the best notes in the world are useless if you can't find them again. Fortunately, Evernote has a powerful search function, so you'll never lose track of a single piece of information. You can structure your notes in a variety of ways and use tags, stacks, and notebooks to organize them. Or you can leave everything free-form. It doesn't matter, because you can search your data so easily that you don't have to focus on structure. Instead, you're free to focus on the fun part: finding your ancestors.

It's Always Available

Evernote works on your desktop computer, your laptop, and your netbook. You can use it on your smartphone or your tablet. In short, it's available everywhere. Even better, your files sync across all your devices, which means you always have an updated copy of all your work at your fingertips.

The Roots of Evernote

Although its features and functions are ideal for family historians, Evernote wasn't designed with genealogists in mind. So how did this tool come about?

The genesis of Evernote was people's universal need to remember stuff (hence the never-forgetting elephant as its symbol). The app was conceived as a way to archive bits and pieces of information from your life—a sort of virtual "brain dump"—and make it possible to retrieve any tidbit lickety-split. Or, as Evernote CEO Phil Libin described his brainchild in *Inc.* magazine, "It's the electronic version of having something at the tip of your tongue."

Evernote launched in 2008, and its fan base has grown steadily ever since: More than 100 million people worldwide use Evernote products. Among them are students, writers, researchers (including genealogists, of course), and those in the business community—Evernote bills itself especially as a productivity-boosting tool.

And it's become more than just the Evernote software. The company offers various add-on apps to extend the core software's usefulness (see chapter 10), plus an Evernote Market of branded products from backpacks and water bottles to gizmos that work seamlessly with Evernote (such as the ScanSnap Evernote Edition scanner).

Twenty Fantastic Free Genealogy Websites

Today you can make amazing progress on your family tree online. Be sure to bookmark these free Internet destinations for genealogy records, user-submitted family trees, old maps, and more—then preserve and organize your finds using Evernote's web clipper (learn more about web clipping in chapter 6).

- AfriGeneas **<www.afrigeneas.com>**
- AncientFaces **<www.ancientfaces.com>**
- BillionGraves **<www.billiongraves.com>**
- Bureau of Land Management General Land Office Records **<www.glorecords.blm.gov>**
- CastleGarden.org **<www.castlegarden.org>**
- Civil War Soldiers and Sailors System **<www.itd.nps.gov/cwss>**
- Cyndi's List **<www.cyndislist.com>**
- Daughters of the American Revolution **<www.dar.org>**
- David Rumsey Historical Maps Collection **<www.davidrumsey.com>**
- FamilySearch.org **<www.familysearch.org>**
- Find A Grave **<www.findagrave.org>**
- GENUKI **<www.genuki.org.uk>**
- JewishGen **<www.jewishgen.org>**
- Library and Archives Canada **<www.bac-lac.gc.ca/eng/Pages/home.aspx>**
- Library of Congress **<www.loc.gov>**
- One-Step Webpages **<www.stevemorse.org>**
- RootsWeb **<rootsweb.ancestry.com>**
- The Statue of Liberty-Ellis Island Foundation **<www.libertyellisfoundation.org>**
- US National Archives and Records Administration **<www.archives.gov>**
- WorldCat **<www.worldcat.org>**

That's helpful because you never know when genealogical inspiration will strike. Have you ever walked through the grocery store, seen a can of Campbell's soup, and remembered that Great-aunt Pearl mentioned a guy named Campbell once? You can enter that tidbit into your Evernote file for follow-up, right there in the soup aisle. Ever driven Great-aunt Pearl to her doctor's appointment and discovered that she's in an uncharacteristically chatty mood? Start recording her ramblings in Evernote right there in the car, and you'll be able to keep them (and find them) years later. Having access to everything all the time opens up a whole new world of opportunity in terms of breaking down brick walls. The smallest clues can lead to the biggest breakthroughs, and now you won't miss a single one.

It's Backed Up in the Cloud

If you've ever booted up your computer and been greeted by the blue screen of death, you know how important backups are. Your Evernote files are backed up in the cloud, so if your computer dies, you can easily access everything from another computer or device in seconds. If you prefer to keep your files backed up locally, you can do that, too. Individual notes can be saved as PDFs, and you can also create backups of entire notebooks. If you really want to protect your data, you can manually back them up, then include them in a folder or directory on your hard drive that's automatically backed up by an online backup service or an external backup drive.

It's Ideal for Collaborating

Sooner or later, most of us end up collaborating with a cousin on a particular family line. Evernote allows you to share notes with your cousin so you can work together. This opens up a world of possibilities. One of you can visit a repository, cemetery, or other location and add notes and other data. That information can be synced and seen by the other cousin in real time. If you've never followed along from three time zones away as your fourth cousin photographs the pages of your common ancestor's Civil War pension file at the National Archives—well, you're in for a treat.

No matter what your level of genealogical experience, Evernote has tools and features to make you better at what you love to do. Ready to get started? In chapter 2, we'll do just that.

KEYS to SUCCESS

✳ Familiarize yourself with the different types of genealogy records and data you can store in Evernote, from notes and photos to audio files and web clippings.

✳ Learn the benefits of using Evernote for your genealogy work, and consider how those advantages will pay dividends in your research.

Getting Started in Evernote

Now that you've gotten a taste of the many benefits to using Evernote for genealogy, you're ready to dive in and get going. In this chapter, we'll walk through the process from start to finish, including how to choose your membership level, create your account, and find your way around the program.

PICKING YOUR PLATFORMS

Your first step in getting set up with Evernote is to choose the platforms on which you'll use the software. Fortunately, you have lots of choices—Evernote works on just about every device you might have. You can use Evernote on

- desktop computers running Windows or Mac OS X;
- laptop computers running Windows or Mac OS X;
- Chromebooks;
- web browsers, including Safari, Chrome, Firefox, and Internet Explorer;
- iOS devices, including the iPad, iPhone, and iPod Touch;
- Android smartphones and tablets;

Evernote works on a variety of platforms and devices. In fact, if you've been holding off on getting a smartphone or tablet, Evernote might be the factor that tips the scales for you. Having all of your data appear on every device is pretty addicting, and it makes life as a genealogist much easier.

- Windows smartphones and tablets; and
- BlackBerry smartphones and tablets.

In short, Evernote probably works on whatever devices you're using (image **A**).

One of the best aspects of Evernote is that it syncs across all devices. That means if you enter one item on your phone, it will automatically appear on your laptop, your desktop, and your tablet. For that reason, you'll get the most out of your Evernote experience if you install it on all of the devices you own. That way, you'll have all of your information at your fingertips, no matter where you are.

Although Evernote works on a wide variety of devices, it's remarkably good at making your experience largely the same on each platform. There are small differences between environments, but for the most part, the major functions are available on every platform. The desktop version (that is, the version you download and install on your own desktop or laptop computer) is the most robust, and that's the best starting point for most users. Throughout this book, we'll be looking at the desktop version of Evernote unless otherwise noted.

TO PAY OR NOT TO PAY?

It's one of the first decisions you'll need to make when you start using Evernote: To pay or not to pay? Like many free software programs and web-based services, Evernote offers upgrade options for a fee. More specifically, Evernote has three user levels (see image **B**):

- Basic membership is free.
- Plus membership costs $2.99 per month, or $24.99 per year.
- Premium membership costs $5.99 per month, or $49.99 per year.

B

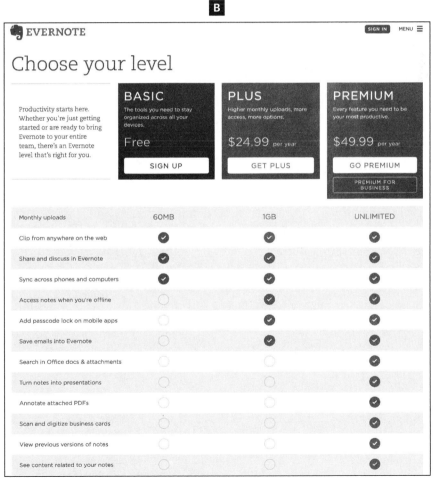

Monthly uploads	60MB	1GB	UNLIMITED
Clip from anywhere on the web	✓	✓	✓
Share and discuss in Evernote	✓	✓	✓
Sync across phones and computers	✓	✓	✓
Access notes when you're offline		✓	✓
Add passcode lock on mobile apps		✓	✓
Save emails into Evernote		✓	✓
Search in Office docs & attachments			✓
Turn notes into presentations			✓
Annotate attached PDFs			✓
Scan and digitize business cards			✓
View previous versions of notes			✓
See content related to your notes			✓

Evernote has three tiers of service: Basic, Plus, and Premium.

To help you decide which option is best for you, let's look at the differences between the three tiers of service within the core Evernote features that you'll use for your genealogy work. Also see the At a Glance: Evernote Features for Genealogists chart for quick reference.

Note Size

Notes, of course, are the essence of Evernote. The free version of Evernote allows up to one hundred thousand notes, with a monthly upload allowance of 60MB. That may sound like a lot, but it's important to remember that photos are usually large files. You could easily use up your entire month's allotment with images from, say, one small Civil War pension file. Plus users have a monthly allowance of 1GB (a far better fit for most genealogists), and Premium users get 10GB per month. In the past, Evernote offered the option to buy additional upload space on a month-to-month basis, but that option was discontinued when the current pricing structure was announced in May 2015.

For individual notes, your maximum size is 25MB for free users, 50MB for Plus users, and 200MB for Premium users. Your total storage amount is unlimited no matter what type of subscription you have; the limits apply only to the amount you can upload in a given month.

Offline Access for Mobile Devices

Users of the free version can access their Evernote files from mobile devices, but only where there's an Internet connection. That's because your data are stored on Evernote's servers, not on your phone or tablet. If you have a Plus or Premium account, you can open your notes even without Internet access—a great benefit for family historians. While Internet access seems practically ubiquitous these days, consider the places you might go while doing research. Cemeteries, for example, rarely have Wi-Fi. At many libraries, the Internet service is so slow that your device can't connect, and I've yet to find a courthouse basement that didn't have a dead spot or two. If you fly to conferences or research destinations, you can avoid having to pay for onboard Wi-Fi in order to access your notes or work on your research plan on your smartphone or tablet.

Sharing

Collaboration is an important part of genealogical research. You can share notes and notebooks with your cousins in the free version of Evernote, but the people you share with won't be able to add to or edit the notes. Plus and Premium subscribers have the opportunity to allow others to read and edit any note or notebook. That's helpful when you're working with a cousin to flesh out your shared connections.

Note History

In the course of doing genealogy research, everyone ends up chasing people who turn out not to be their ancestors: You investigate a branch from an online family tree that wasn't thoroughly researched, or you follow three separate Hugh Humperdinks in your ancestral county because you don't know which one is your Hugh. Sometimes you wonder where you got off track or realize you deleted something seemingly irrelevant that turned out to be a major clue.

Premium Evernote users have access to a feature called Note History. This allows you to see changes to your document, sorted by date, so you can figure out exactly where you went wrong (and restore your old notes, if necessary). It's like having an Undo button that goes back for years. Plus and Basic users don't have the Note History feature.

Presentation Mode

It's hard to get nongenealogists interested in our discoveries. We understand the thrill of finding our third great-grandmother's maiden name, but our relatives don't always get it. One way we can reel them in is by presenting our results in exciting, engaging ways. Evernote Premium users have a Presentation Mode feature that works similar to a PowerPoint slide show (but without the hassle and expense of actually using PowerPoint). It's a great way to make family reunions or Thanksgiving dinners more exciting. If you volunteer with your local genealogical or historical society, this can be handy for meetings as well. This feature is not available for Basic or Plus users.

PDF Searching and Annotating

All Evernote users have the ability to search inside a regular text-based PDF (one generated from a word processing program or an e-mail, for instance). But what about image-based PDFs generated through scanning an image or document? Genealogists use these often, and only Premium users can search within those as well.

Think about the types of PDFs you have in your collection. For example, you might request a copy of an obituary from the local library where your ancestors lived. The library will send you an image of that obituary from the newspaper; it won't be retyped for you. If you're a Premium subscriber, that image will be completely searchable when you drop it into Evernote.

You might also inherit the research done by a previous generation, including lots of documents you'll want to scan and convert to PDF for safekeeping. You might even have digital copies of reference magazines such as *Family Tree Magazine*, with years' worth of helpful articles—if you can find them. Having these types of documents converted to an instantly searchable document without any effort on your part is a huge time-saver, and that additional functionality is available only to Premium subscribers. Additionally, Premium users can annotate PDFs, which is a huge help when you have a hard-to-read document and need to highlight key points or want to call attention to something important. We'll talk much more about these features in chapter 6.

Related Notes

Have you ever begun working on an ancestor, spent lots of time on research, then had a strange sense of déjà vu? It's not just you. Even the best researchers can end up duplicating efforts, forgetting about work done years ago, or failing to realize the connection between two discoveries made years apart. Evernote's Related Notes feature for Premium subscribers can help by automatically alerting you when a new note seems to relate to something you've done in the past. The more you use Evernote, the better this feature works. This feature is for Premium subscribers only; it's not available for Basic or Plus accounts.

Passcode Lock for Mobile Devices

Depending on what you plan to keep in your Evernote file, it might make sense to have a passcode to keep it from prying eyes. I use Evernote for genealogical research, but I also use it for things related to my young descendants (including a list of the items Santa's bought for them). One of my kids is a snooper—which I'm hoping points to a future in genealogy—so I keep my Evernote file locked down during the holiday season. That way, I can be sure that if I hand over my phone to make a long wait at the doctor's office go faster, I won't be giving away Santa's secrets. You can set a passcode lock if you have a Plus or Premium subscription, but it's not an option for Basic subscribers.

Saving E-Mails Into Evernote

E-mail is a huge component of any genealogist's toolbox, and it has been for decades. Nearly every family historian has a collection of e-mails from distant cousins, relatives who are no longer with us, and other genealogical collaborators. Plus and Premium users have the option of sending those e-mails directly into Evernote, where they'll be stored, backed up, and made searchable. You can then tag them with the surnames, locations, or records they relate to. This is also a great tool for the myriad of genealogy-related newsletters you may subscribe to. You can store and save those in Evernote as well, so they're easier to find when you need them. The e-mail-to-Evernote feature is not available for Basic subscribers, but Plus and Premium subscribers can save up to two hundred e-mails per day.

At a Glance: Evernote Features for Genealogists

	Basic Account	Plus Account	Premium Account
Cost	free	$2.99 per month or $24.99 per year	$5.99 per month or $49.99 per year
Monthly upload limit	60MB	1GB	10GB
Maximum individual note size	25MB (about two Civil War pension files)	50MB (about four Civil War pension files)	200MB (about sixteen Civil War pension files)
Offline access	desktop/laptop only	desktop/laptop plus phone/tablet	desktop/laptop plus phone/tablet
Sharing options	read-only sharing	read/edit sharing	read/edit sharing
Note history	no	no	yes
Presentation mode	no	no	yes
PDF annotating	no	no	yes
PDF searching	no	no	yes
Related notes	no	no	yes
Passcode lock	no	no	yes
Saving e-mails	no	200 per day	200 per day
Support via e-mail	no	yes	yes
Support via live chat	no	no	yes

Premium Concierge

Got questions? Premium subscribers have the option of getting help via a live chat. You'll be connected with real humans who are Evernote experts. It's a great resource when you're stuck. Plus subscribers can put in a support ticket via e-mail and get help that way, but they don't have access to live chat. Basic users have access to community support only.

As you can see, there are some big advantages to having an Evernote Plus or Premium subscription, especially for genealogical use. If you're still not sure, try the free version first and see if you miss the extra functions, space, and support. You might find the free version adequate for getting started, then decide to upgrade once you're comfortable with the program and want to do more with it.

SETTING UP YOUR EVERNOTE ACCOUNT

Whether you decide to go with a free or a paid subscription, your first step will be to set up an Evernote account. Just follow this simple process:

1. Go to <**www.evernote.com**>.

2. Click the green Sign up now button.

3. Enter the e-mail address and password you want to use for your Evernote account. Keep in mind that the e-mail address you use will be the one where you'll receive Evernote news and announcements.

Adjusting Your Settings

Once you've signed up, you'll end up on the main Evernote screen. The first thing you'll want to do is set up your account with your name and adjust your settings to your liking. Here's how to do this:

1. Find the circle button with your first initial in it in the lower left corner. Click it.

2. A pop-up menu will appear. Click Settings.

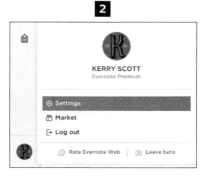

3. You'll land on the Account Summary page. See the part where it says E-mail Notes to at the bottom? There will be a strange-looking e-mail address next to that with part of your real e-mail address, plus a series of random letters and numbers. Make a note of that special e-mail address, because we'll be using it in chapter 6. If you forget what it is, you can always find it on this Account Summary page.

4. Click Personal Settings in the top left portion of your screen. This will take you to a page where you can put in your full name, choose your display language, and choose your "Recognition Language." This little-known feature is a real boon to genealogists. It allows you to choose one language in addition to English, which will be used when Evernote indexes images and PDFs. If you take a photo of, say, an obituary, Evernote will index every word in that obituary, so you can find it again using the search feature. With an additional Recognition Language selection, you're telling Evernote to do this in a second language as well. If you work with foreign-language

3

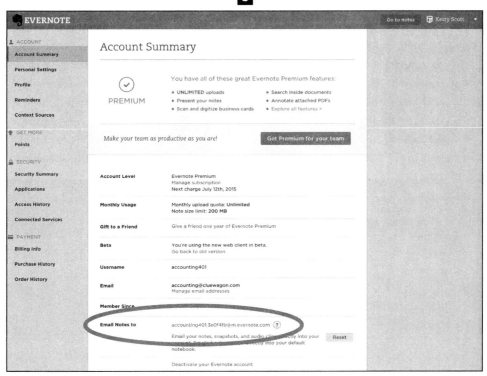

4

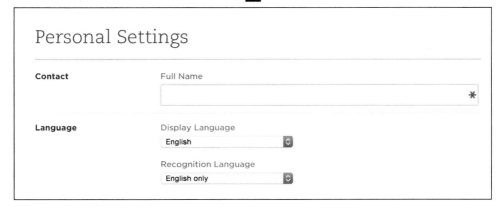

newspapers or other records, this can be a real game changer. Your second-language choices include

- Arabic
- Catalan
- Croatian
- Czech
- Danish
- Dutch
- Estonian
- Finish
- French
- German
- Greek
- Hungarian
- Indonesian
- Italian
- Japanese

5

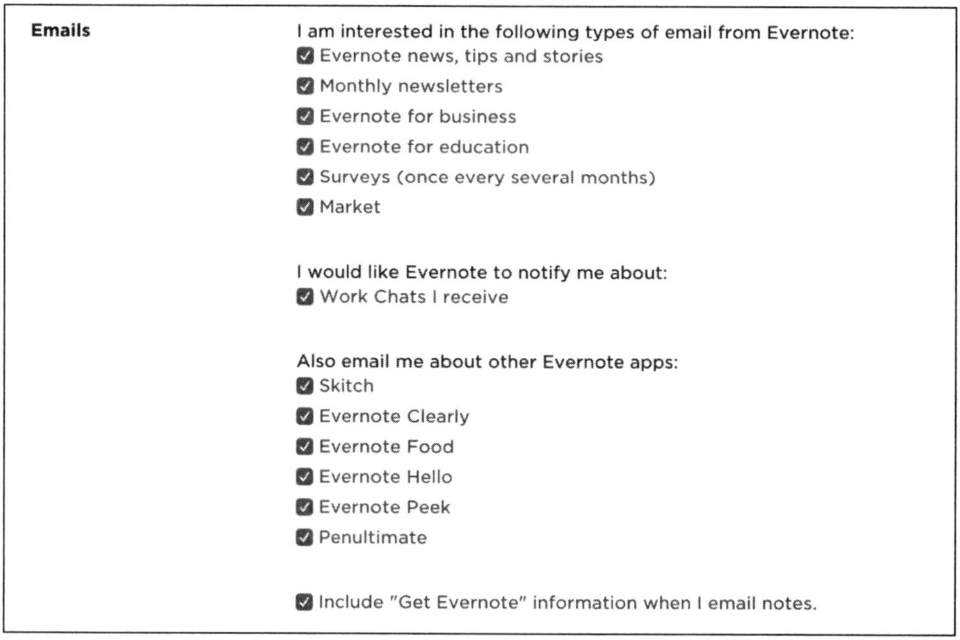

Emails	I am interested in the following types of email from Evernote:
	☑ Evernote news, tips and stories
	☑ Monthly newsletters
	☑ Evernote for business
	☑ Evernote for education
	☑ Surveys (once every several months)
	☑ Market
	I would like Evernote to notify me about:
	☑ Work Chats I receive
	Also email me about other Evernote apps:
	☑ Skitch
	☑ Evernote Clearly
	☑ Evernote Food
	☑ Evernote Hello
	☑ Evernote Peek
	☑ Penultimate
	☑ Include "Get Evernote" information when I email notes.

- Korean
- Mandarin
- Norwegian
- Polish
- Portuguese
- Romanian
- Russian
- Serbian
- Spanish
- Swedish
- Turkish

5. From the Personal Settings page, you can also choose what types of e-mails you want to receive from Evernote. If you're a beginner, it's a good idea to sign up for the newsletters, which offer a variety of helpful tips.

DOWNLOADING EVERNOTE TO YOUR COMPUTER AND DEVICES

To get the most out of Evernote (and this book), you'll want to download the software to your desktop or laptop computer. To do that, you'll go back to the Evernote website, then click the Download button at the top of the page. Evernote will automatically detect your operating system. Depending on your computer's settings, it may automatically begin downloading, or it may prompt you to do so. From here, you'll need to follow the installation instructions that work for your specific computer setup. Generally speaking, on a Windows computer, you'll double-click on the file you downloaded to begin the installation process. On a Mac, you'll drag that file to the Applications folder to start installing.

To install Evernote on your other devices, visit the place you normally buy apps for that specific device. Here's where to look for each type of device:

- Android devices: Google Play store
- BlackBerry devices: BlackBerry App World
- iPhone, iPad, or iPod Touch: App Store
- Kindle Fire: Amazon Appstore
- Windows phones: Microsoft Store Marketplace

POWER-USER TIP

Using Multiple Devices
You can install Evernote on as many devices as you like. Just be sure to sign in with the same login information to ensure they're all attached to the same account. That will enable your data to sync across all devices.

MAKING SENSE OF THE MAIN SCREEN

The first time you open Evernote on your desktop or laptop, you'll find a screen that displays a great deal of white space. That can be intimidating to new users, and sometimes it's hard to know where to start. Let's review each part of the screen, working clockwise from the top left. For easy reference, each feature is labeled on image **C**.

1 Your name is the place to click in order to access your account information, including your billing and subscription data, your e-mail address, and your usage information. This is handy if you're tracking how much of your data upload allotment has been used so far this month, as well as how many days you have left before your allotment rolls over.

2 The sync button allows you to manually sync your data across all devices. Unless you have an urgent need to sync immediately, this usually isn't necessary, but it's nice to have the option. Evernote will automatically sync for you every fifteen minutes.

3 The little satellite button connects you to your notifications. You'll receive those when there's new stuff in your shared notebooks.

4 The New Note button is, as the name implies, the place you'll go to create a new note. Hold that thought, because we'll come back to that in the next section.

5 New Chat (and its companion, **Work Chat**) is designed to allow work groups to collaborate using text chat. It works similarly to Google Chat or your smartphone's texting app (although it doesn't use up your cellular plan's texting allotment, even if you're actually using it on your phone). It's not used much by genealogists, but it's an interesting tool to explore if you're working with cousins or fellow genealogical society members.

6 Search notes is a place you'll be spending lots of time. This is where the main search function for Evernote lives, and it's full of power. We'll come back to it in chapter 4, once we have some notes to search.

7 All Notes takes you to a complete list of all of your notes. By default, they'll be listed in reverse chronological order, so your most recent note will be at the top. You'll fill this up in no time.

8 Announcements is where you'll find news from Evernote itself. Watch this space for information about new and improved features, new releases and apps, and other important information.

9 Premium or **Upgrade** is where you can view or upgrade your subscription. If you already have a Premium account, this link will connect you to the Premium Concierge, where you can chat live with help desk professionals and get your questions answered.

10 Market is a link to Evernote's own shop. There, you can find a selection of accessories for Evernote users. From laptop bags to fancy water bottles to Moleskine notebooks to forty-dollar pencil cups, you'll find them here.

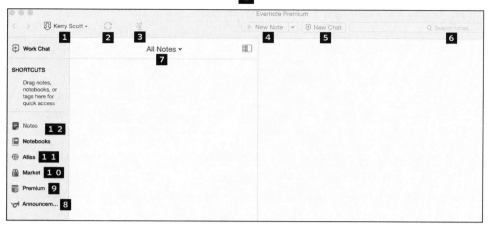

The main Evernote screen is your jumping-off point for accessing Evernote's tools and features.

11 Atlas is where you can see all of your notes on a map. If you've allowed Evernote to use your location, it will geotag your notes. This is handy for genealogy tasks such as cemetery research. We'll cover this in greater detail in chapter 5.

12 Notebooks and **Notes** are where you'll find your own stuff. We'll talk more about these organizational tools in chapter 3.

CREATING YOUR FIRST NOTE

Ready to start? Here's how to create your first note in Evernote:

1. Click the New Note button.

2. Evernote will ask you if it's okay to "use your current location." This allows it to geotag your notes so that you can find them by location. That means your notes taken at home will show up on the map, along with those taken on your research trips, at your grandparents' family farm, at your favorite genealogical library, and so forth. It's a great tool if you want to be able to find all of the notes from a specific research trip. If you want to enable this feature, click OK. If you're not comfortable with geotagging, click Don't Allow.

3. You'll see the word *Untitled* near the top, on the left-hand side. That's the note title field. Click there, then type whatever title you like over it.

4. Click the spot where you see "Drag files here or just start typing." That's your starting point. Type whatever you like.

Note Know-How

Here are a few additional things you should know about creating a note.

- The notes entry screen resembles a word processing or e-mail document. You can change the font, the font size, and other text characteristics using the ribbon at the top. To do this, highlight the text you want to change, then click the relevant button and make your selection. If you want to make several words of text boldface, for example, click the B button.

- You can create bullets and numbered lists, and create tables, a feature we'll use quite a bit when we discuss research logs in chapter 8.

- There's a microphone button to record audio files and a camera-shutter button to take a photo with your computer's webcam. We'll cover these in more detail in chapter 6.

- The paper clip button is for attaching files (including PDFs, Microsoft Office files, and more) to Evernote notes.

- Above the toolbar, you'll notice a little tag. Tags are an especially powerful tool for genealogists—not just for organizing, but for analyzing your data and spotting patterns that help you break down brick walls. We'll cover tags in depth in chapter 5.

Congratulations! You've just become an Evernote user. Your genealogical life just got easier. It's customary to celebrate this achievement with ice cream.

KEYS to SUCCESS

* Give some thought to how you'll use Evernote. While Plus and Premium subscriptions cost more, you'll get a lot more bang for your genealogical buck.

* Remember that you can choose to pay your subscription monthly instead of annually. This might be a more budget-friendly option for some users.

* After you've set up your account, download Evernote onto every device you use regularly. This ensures that your data will be available wherever and whenever you need them.

* Take the time to go through the personal settings, especially the Recognition Language feature, which is a real boon to genealogists.

* After you create your first note, explore some of your editing options. The best way to get familiar with this new tool is to play with it a bit.

EVERNOTE SETUP CHECKLIST AND WORKSHEET

Before Creating Your Account

☐ Using the At a Glance chart in this chapter, review the features of Evernote Basic, Plus, and Premium accounts. Note the features that are most important to you and your genealogy needs.

_____

_____

_____

_____

_____

_____

☐ Decide which type of account you'll sign up for. Account type: _____

After Creating Your Account

☐ Record your login information so you'll have it handy for setup on your other devices.

My Evernote user name: _____

My Evernote password (or a password hint):_____

Payment type:_____ Monthly/Annual:_____

Next payment date (if monthly, note the day of the month):_____

☐ Adjust your account settings as you wish, including opting in or out of geotagging.

☐ Download Evernote to all applicable devices:

    ☐ desktop computer

    ☐ laptop computer

    ☐ tablet computer (iPad, Kindle Fire, Microsoft Surface, etc.)

    ☐ smartphone

☐ Create your first note and test out the note-editing functions.

Organizing in Evernote

Remember when you first started using a computer? You had to spend a great deal of time thinking about how to organize your files, because if you didn't put stuff in the right place, you might never find it again. Should you file your ancestors by surname? What about those whose surnames you don't know yet or those who changed surnames frequently? Or should you file your ancestors by location? What if the location name changed? What happens when you don't know where they're from? After all, we all have ancestors who seem to have beamed down from outer space. Where on Earth would you file them?

Thankfully, times have changed. Computers have gotten more sophisticated, and it's much easier to search for our electronic files. Evernote has a robust search feature, and that means it's much easier to stay organized and find what you're looking for. In fact, if you're one of those people who hates to even think about organizing things, fear not. You could put every single tidbit you find into Evernote notes, with no other organizational system at all, and it's highly likely that you'd still find it again.

Most of us, though, like to have a bit more structure to our stuff. Evernote's organizational structure is quite simple, but that simplicity comes with a great deal of flexibility.

Everyone's brain works differently, and that flexibility allows you to create just the right setup to meet your individual needs. It's also easy to change your mind and create a whole new structure on the fly. You can even use different strategies for different projects and cross-reference them using tags (more on this in chapter 5).

Evernote has three basic levels of organization: notes, notebooks, and stacks. Let's take a quick look at each one.

NOTES

Notes are the heart of Evernote. They're the place where you can type in text; add photos of people, things, and documents; add attachments; and record audio files (image 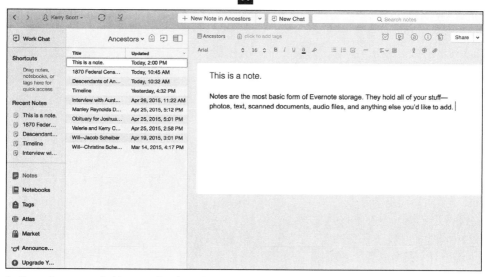). In short, they're the container that holds all the good stuff inside. You can have up to 25MB of data in an individual note if you're using the Basic (free) version of Evernote, 50MB of data if you're a Plus subscriber, or 200MB of data if you're a Premium subscriber.

You can have a variety of types of data in an individual note. Text, photos, audio files, web clippings—they can all go in the same note, in whatever order you like (or in no order at all). Keep in mind, though, that some photos and most audio files are large. You can easily hit the individual note limits with even a fairly small audio file. For that reason, you'll want to consider investing in one of the paid subscription options if you want to get the most out of your Evernote experience.

A

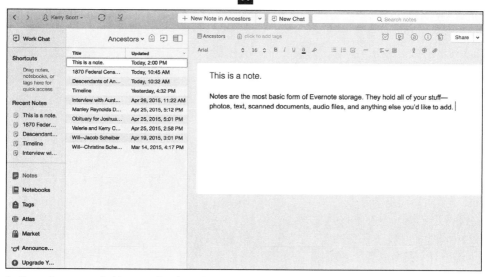

An Evernote note can hold text and multimedia attachments.

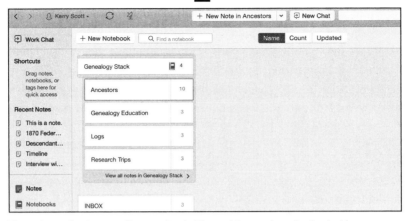

The main notebook screen lists notebook titles and the number of notes inside.

Notes will have titles, of course, and the text within them is fully searchable. If you're a Premium subscriber, the text within photos and scanned PDFs is also searchable. Additionally, you can add up to one hundred tags to each note (although that's probably too many to be useful). We'll cover tags in greater detail in chapter 5.

NOTEBOOKS

Notebooks (image **B**) are essentially a collection of notes. You can create notebooks for just about anything, and you can have up to 250 notebooks per account. Here's how to create a notebook:

1. From your main Evernote screen, click the Notebooks link on the left-hand side.

2. At the top of your screen, click the New Notebook button.

3. You'll be prompted to type in a name for your notebook. Hit return after you've entered a name you like.

That's all there is to it. Easy, right?

Managing Stacks and Notebooks

To see your management options for notebooks and stacks, hover your mouse over the one you want, then right-click. From there, you can rename the item, delete it, or change the order in which items appear. If you want to view all notes in a particular stack (regardless of which notebook they're in), click the link at the bottom of the list of notebooks in that stack.

STACKS

A stack is a group of notebooks (see image **C**). In genealogical terms, if notes are the main characters, notebooks would be their parents, and stacks would be their grandparents. Follow the steps below to create a stack:

1. From your main Evernote screen, click the Notebooks link on the left-hand side.

2. Review your list of notebooks (you'll need at least two notebooks to do this). Hover your mouse over one notebook, click and hold your mouse button, and drag that notebook on top of the notebook you want to pair it with to create a stack.

3. Your stack will automatically name itself. To change the name to something more meaningful, hover your mouse over the name of the stack, then right-click (control-click on Macs). Select Rename Stack and type in the name you want to use. Hit return, and it'll show up with the new name.

C

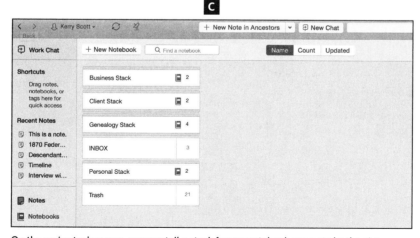

On the main stack screen, you can tell a stack from a notebook or a note by the picture of a binder to the right of the stack name. The number next to it indicates the number of notebooks in that stack.

Does Your Device Stack Up?

Stacks are not available on all platforms. BlackBerry users and Windows Phone users do not have access to stacks. Stacks do work on the web version of Evernote, on the Mac and Windows desktop versions, and on both iOS and Android devices. Stacks are not shareable—only individual notes and notebooks can be shared with others. We'll cover sharing in detail in chapter 7.

HOW TO USE NOTES, NOTEBOOKS, AND STACKS FOR GENEALOGY

There are so many ways to organize your research in Evernote that you might feel flummoxed about where to start. In fact, some researchers find this step absolutely paralyzing, because they're afraid of getting it wrong. If that's you, relax.

The beauty of Evernote is that it doesn't matter too much how you structure your notes. The powerful search feature means it's extremely likely you'll be able to find what you're looking for, even if you can't remember where you filed it. You can also change your mind and completely redesign your entire organization scheme just by dragging your notes and notebooks around. You can reorganize your Evernote files way faster than you can reorganize your old file cabinet (and you won't get paper cuts or start sneezing from the dust either).

That said, there are some obvious possibilities for how you might like to set up your genealogy note-keeping scheme: by record type, by family branch, or by activity or project. Let's take a peek at these options.

Example: Organizing by Record Type

Much of genealogy research revolves around searching for and obtaining records of your ancestors, so you may want to organize information around those records. Here's what organizing by record type might look like:

STACK 1: Census Records

    Notebook 1: Federal census

- Note 1: 1790 Census notes
- Note 2: 1800 Census notes
- Note 3: 1810 Census notes

    Notebook 2: State census—Minnesota

- Note 1: 1865 Census
- Note 2: 1875 Census
- Note 3: 1885 Census

Notebook 3: State census—Iowa

- Note 1: 1885 Census
- Note 2: 1895 Census
- Note 3: 1905 Census

STACK 2: Vital Records

Notebook 1: Birth records

- Note 1: Birth certificate for John Smith
- Note 2: Birth certificate for Mary Jones
- Note 3: Birth certificate for Joseph Redfeather

Notebook 2: Marriage records

- Note 1: Marriage record for Nels Nelson and Kristine Erickson
- Note 2: Marriage record for Sigmund Cohen and Henrietta Schwartz
- Note 3: Marriage record for Johann Meier and Anna Marie Leiendecker

Notebook 3: Death records

- Note 1: Death record for Juan Garcia
- Note 2: Death record for Kenji Shinosake
- Note 3: Death record for Mary O'Shea

Example: Organizing by Family Branch

Some genealogists find it natural to keep mental tabs on information by person or family, and you can certainly set up Evernote to reflect that. A scheme of organizing by family branch might look like this:

STACK 1: My Paternal Grandparents

Notebook 1: Joseph Blow, my paternal grandfather

- Note 1: Joseph Blow's birth, marriage, and death records
- Note 2: Joseph Blow's census records
- Note 3: Joseph Blow's probate and land records

Notebook 2: Jane Dough, my paternal grandmother

- Note 1: Jane Dough's birth, marriage, and death records
- Note 2: Jane Dough's census records
- Note 3: Jane Dough's probate and land records

STACK 2: My Maternal Grandparents

Notebook 1: Iver Iverson, my paternal grandfather

- Note 1: Iver Iverson's birth, marriage, and death records
- Note 2: Iver Iverson's census records
- Note 3: Iver Iverson's probate and land records

Notebook 2: Lena Larsdatter, my paternal grandmother

- Note 1: Lena Larsdatter's birth, marriage, and death records
- Note 2: Lena Larsdatter's census records
- Note 3: Lena Larsdatter's probate and land records

Of course, you could vary your level of grandparent-hood. You could have a stack for each of your four grandparents, your eight great-grandparents, or your sixteen great-great-grandparents. Keep in mind that you can share a notebook, but you can't share a whole stack. For that reason, if you envision collaborating with cousins on a common family line, you'll probably want that branch to be covered by a notebook rather than a stack.

Example: Organizing by Activity or Project

In addition to records and people, genealogists also like to keep tabs on particular research projects and activities, such as research trips, logs, and learning. Organizing by genealogy activity would look similar to this example:

STACK 1: My Genealogical Education

Notebook 1: Family Tree University courses

- Note 1: Irish 101 course
- Note 2: German 201 course
- Note 3: Using Evernote course

Notebook 2: Salt Lake Institute of Genealogy

- Note 1: Eastern European course
- Note 2: Research in the South course
- Note 3: Advanced Genealogical Methods course

STACK 2: My Logs

Notebook 1: My correspondence log

- Note 1: Items ordered online
- Note 2: Items ordered via mail
- Note 3: Items ordered in person

Notebook 2: Marriage records

- Note 1: Research log for my maternal lines
- Note 2: Research log for my paternal lines
- Note 3: Research log for FANs (friends, associates, and neighbors)

STACK 3: My Research Trips

Notebook 1: Trip to Minneapolis, July 2016

- Note 1: Travel information (flight, hotel, etc.)

- Note 2: Research plan (with list of records to pull)
- Note 3: Research notes
- Note 4: Ancestral homes or other sites to find
- Note 5: Restaurants and things to do

Notebook 2: Trip to Salt Lake City, January 2017

- Note 1: Travel information (flight, hotel, etc.)
- Note 2: Research plan (with list of records to pull)
- Note 3: Research notes
- Note 4: Ancestral homes or other sites to find
- Note 5: Restaurants and things to do

Notebook 3: Trip to Milwaukee, June 2017

- Note 1: Travel information (flight, hotel, etc.)
- Note 2: Research plan (with list of records to pull)
- Note 3: Research notes
- Note 4: Ancestral homes or other sites to find
- Note 5: Restaurants and things to do

STACK 4: My DNA Stuff

Notebook 1: My chromosome matches

- Note 1: Chromosome 1
- Note 2: Chromosome 2
- Notes 3–22: Chromosomes 3-22
- Note 23: X Chromosome

Notebook 2: GEDmatch info

- Note 1: Kit numbers of known cousins
- Note 2: My latest one-to-many report
- Note 3: My latest matching segment report
- Note 4: My latest triangulation report
- Note 5: Relationship tree projections for matches

Notebook 3: Admixture info

- Note 1: My ethnicity predictions from 23andMe
- Note 2: My ethnicity predictions from Family Tree DNA
- Note 3: My ethnicity predictions from AncestryDNA

Notebook 4: Correspondence log

- Note 1: Cousins I've contacted on 23andMe
- Note 2: Cousins I've contacted on Family Tree DNA
- Note 3: Cousins I've contacted on AncestryDNA

Choosing Your Organizational Structure

Of course, you aren't limited to just one of the above systems—you might adopt parts of those and make up more of your own. Some of your organizational structure decisions will relate to your specific research goals, your ethnic heritage, and the specific needs of your ancestral lines. As you ponder what structure works for you, consider these factors:

- Surnames are a great way to organize—for some people. For other researchers, they're useless. If you have colonial heritage, you probably have enough Smith lines to form a baseball team (or maybe even a whole league). If you're Scandinavian, you're dealing with patronyms (surnames based on the father's given name, such as Lena Larsdatter—

Seven Space-Saving Strategies

Genealogists can't help collecting stuff—we accumulate piles upon piles of records, printouts, and ephemera while chasing ancestors. Using Evernote as a central system to organize all your genealogy materials will make your collection more accessible, but how do you tame the paper tiger? Follow these hints from *Family Tree Magazine* to cut clutter in your work space:

1. *Search for digitized versions of large reference books.* Not only can you search an e-book to find what you're looking for quickly, you can easily tote it along on your laptop or desktop during research outings.

2. *Digitize whenever possible.* Purchase back issues of magazines and journals on spacesaving CDs, consider digital magazine subscriptions, and opt for digital conference syllabi.

3. *Purge papers you don't need and set up a filing system for the rest.* Learn more about genealogy paper filing systems in the free e-book *23 Secrets to Organize Your Genealogy*, available from **<www.familytreemagazine.com/family-tree-tips-23-secrets-to-organize-your-genealogy>**.

4. *Keep only the heirlooms that are meaningful to you and give the rest to relatives.* Don't feel guilty about donating or tossing "artifacts" that relatives don't want—just be sure to take pictures to incorporate the items into your family's record.

5. *Print photos and scanned documents judiciously.* You don't need a hard copy of every image on your hard drive. Choose a few cherished snapshots for display or feature your favorites in a photo book.

6. *Organize family photos in archival albums or storage containers.* Store oddly shaped heirlooms in boxes sized to fit.

7. *Record your family history in a special place so family will recognize its value.* You could use a keepsake journal such as *Family Tree Memory Keeper* by Allison Dolan and Diane Haddad (Family Tree Books), or create a quick-and-easy photo book of family pictures and documents using Shutterfly **<www.shutterfly.com>** or a similar service.

meaning Lena, the daughter of Lars). In that case, the farm name might actually make a better label. (If the family stuck to the farm name, that is. Mine didn't. Mine seemed to change their name whenever they changed their underwear. Here's hoping yours were more understanding of the needs of future genealogists.) If you have Hispanic heritage, you'll be dealing with multiple surnames for the same person, because women kept their maiden names and appended their husbands' family names after marriage.

- Adoptees and others with unknown paternity/maternity have special challenges when it comes to genealogy. If you're using DNA to help sort this out, you might want to have a notebook for each chromosome, then include notes on those matches.

- You may find that as you use Evernote more and more, you discover uses for it outside of genealogy. Keep in mind that your organizational structure might change as you begin to incorporate other parts of your life into your Evernote file.

Again, this is where Evernote's flexibility comes in handy: You needn't worry about creating one perfect system. It's easy to adapt and change your setup on the fly.

My Evernote Organization Scheme

Though I started using Evernote specifically for my genealogical research, it wasn't long before it took over my life. Here's how I structure my own Evernote files:

- **Personal Stack:** This contains everything related to the running of my household and family. From our grocery list to menus for holidays to notes on the paint colors in our home, it's all here. When my family moved from Milwaukee to Albuquerque, I had a shared notebook related to the move. That way, my husband could access my notes and find information when he needed it, and we could be sure we were both on the same page (literally). It kept us sane through a cross-country move with two small children and a tight time frame.

- **Business Stack:** This is where I keep things related to my own business. I take photos of receipts for tax purposes and store them here; my list of potential article and blog post ideas lives in this stack, too.

- **Client Stack:** Any information that belongs to someone else goes in this stack. In some cases, I share the individual notebooks with the client in question (so it's important that data do not mingle).

- **Genealogy Stack:** My own genealogical notes are all here. Inside I keep my research and correspondence logs, my notes from conferences I've attended, and my information on lines I'm researching. When I do on-site research, all of my findings go into this stack. I don't structure it too much because I know I can easily find any item I want using the Evernote search feature.

MORE ORGANIZING TOOLS IN EVERNOTE

In addition to allowing you a great deal of flexibility in the way you structure information, Evernote offers additional tools to keep you organized.

Shortcuts and Recent Notes

When you're on the main Evernote screen, you'll notice a section called Shortcuts on the top left side (see image **D**). This is a spot where you can drag notes, notebooks, or even stacks for easy access. Shortcuts are especially handy for stuff you use all the time, such as your research and correspondence logs. Right below your shortcuts, you'll find a list of Recent Notes. As the name implies, this is a list of the notes you've worked with most recently in reverse chronological order. If you can't figure out what you just did with your note, check this spot. You'll probably find what you're looking for.

Reminders

Believe it or not, Evernote can remind you to do stuff, just like your favorite calendar app. This is a great way to ensure that you stay on task and don't get sidetracked by a shiny new ancestor. It's also helpful if you're dealing with record restrictions. For example, if you have a relative who died in Oregon in July 1968, you won't be able to order her death certificate until fifty years have passed (that's the state law in Oregon). You can set a reminder for July 2018 so you remember to order that death certificate the second it's available.

Reminders are also great if you're on a budget. You might want to order a bunch of microfilm via interlibrary loan, for example. Because the cost for this can really add up, you might want to spread it out. You can set reminders for which microfilm rolls you want to order each month so you stay on budget. As a side benefit, this also helps you budget your

D

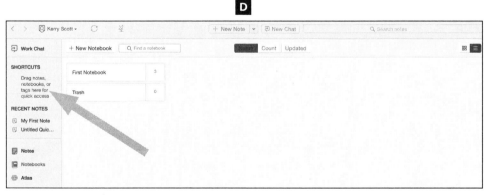

Drag notes to the top left area labeled Shortcuts for easy access.

time: You can space out your requests at intervals roughly equivalent to the time you'll have to send the microfilm back to its original lending library.

Here's how to set up a reminder for a note:

1. Navigate to the note that relates to the reminder item.

2. Click the little clock symbol at the top of your note (see image **E**).

3. If you don't want to assign your reminder to a specific date, you're done. Your reminder will be visible on the Reminders list near your notes.

4. If you want to choose a date, use the dialog box (image **F**) to scroll through the calendar to select a day. There are shortcut buttons for Tomorrow and Next Week.

E

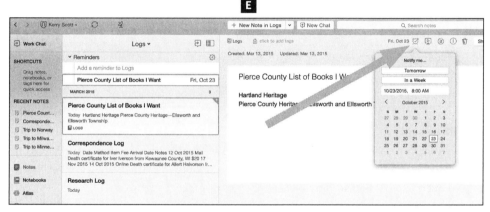

Log items on the Reminders screen for quick reference.

F

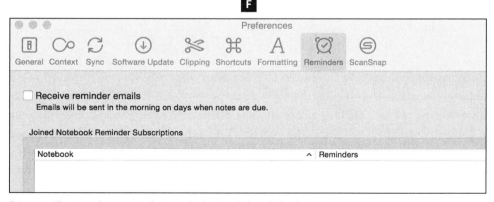

Set up notifications for your to-do items in the Reminders dialog box.

Prioritizing With Reminders

Like most genealogists, I have a list of records and resources I want, and it far exceeds my actual genealogy budget. I keep a list of the more expensive books and records I want to order, sorted by priority. Then I use the Reminder feature to remind me to order them once my direct deposit hits. This helps keep me from blowing my entire month's genealogy budget on one late-night pension-ordering binge (you've been there, right?).

5. You'll be prompted to decide whether you want to receive an e-mail reminder or not. If not, you'll receive reminders in the Evernote app, and you'll see a badge on the app tile on your mobile device (this is the little red number signaling that you have messages or notifications waiting). On a Mac, your desktop icon will also show a red notification badge if you have reminders waiting.

6. Click outside the dialog box to save the note.

To mark a reminder item complete, click on the little clock symbol again. If you want to change the sort order of your reminders or adjust your default preferences for notifications, click the gear icon on the right-hand side of the Reminders menu bar.

To-Do Lists

Sometimes it's hard to stay on task when you're doing genealogical research. It's so easy to be attracted by a new find, a new ancestor, or a new resource. To-do lists are a great way to keep yourself focused and so you don't wander off and miss a step.

G

INBOX   click to add tags

Created: Mar 14, 2015   Updated: Mar 14, 2015

To-Do List

☑ Write book on Evernote genealogy
☐ Trace ancestors back to Adam and Eve
☐ Take a nap

Creating to-do lists with checkboxes in Evernote is easy.

You can create a to-do list simply by making a note, then typing out the list of things you want to include. Of course, there's nothing more satisfying than checking off the items as you complete them, and Evernote has a checkbox feature to allow you to do this (see image **G**). Here's how to use it:

1. Create a note for your to-do list (or, alternatively, open an existing note related to a project or ancestor where you want to track your to-do items).

2. Type out a list of items you want to accomplish.

3. Position your mouse at the beginning of the first item. Click the checkbox icon in the toolbar at the top to insert a checkbox.

4. That's it. When you've completed a task, click the box to check it off the list, then pause to congratulate yourself on your productivity.

You can use this feature for a variety of genealogical purposes. Consider making a master packing list for your research trips or a list of items to take with you when you visit the library. You could also make a list of genealogical books or other things you want so you have it handy when your spouse asks, "What do you want for your birthday?" In fact, you could even share the note with the list directly with your gift givers. You'll learn more about sharing in chapter 7.

DIFFERENT WAYS TO VIEW YOUR DATA

Part of staying organized in Evernote is figuring out the right way to view your data. Screen views are like bathing suits: You have to try out a few to see which one fits you best. To change your view, either choose View from the top menu, then make your selection, or click the View icon at the top of your note list. You have five different choices:

Snippet View

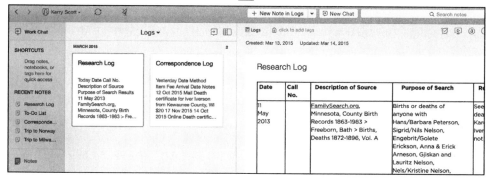

Card View

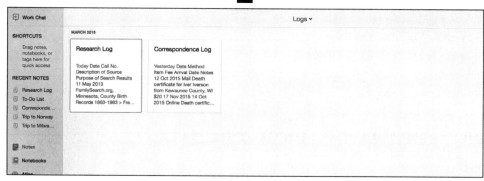

Expanded Card View

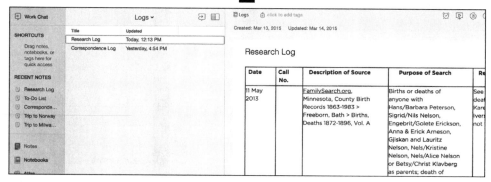

Side List View

How to Use Evernote for Genealogy

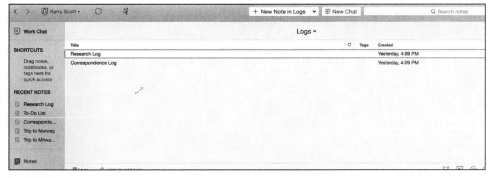

Top List View

- Snippet View (the default, image ■H■)
- Card View (image ■I■)
- Expanded Card View (image ■J■)
- Side List View (image ■K■)
- Top List View (image ■L■)

Within each view, you have the option to sort by the following parameters:

- Title
- Date Created
- Date Updated
- Source URL
- Size

MAKING CHANGES

As your use of Evernote increases, it's likely that your organizational structure will evolve over time and may transform depending on what you're working on. In Evernote, it's easy to move, rename, or delete material.

Moving/Copying an Item

To move an item, you can hover your mouse over it, right-click, then choose Move to Notebook or Copy to Notebook (see image ■M■). Alternatively, you can drag

This menu appears when you right-click on a note.

Retrieving Deleted Notes

If you've deleted something by mistake,
don't panic. Your Evernote account
comes with a notebook called Trash,
and that's the cemetery for deleted
notes. Click on it, find your note, then
click Restore Note. Voilà! Your note will
return to its original home. If only we
could do this in real cemeteries.

N

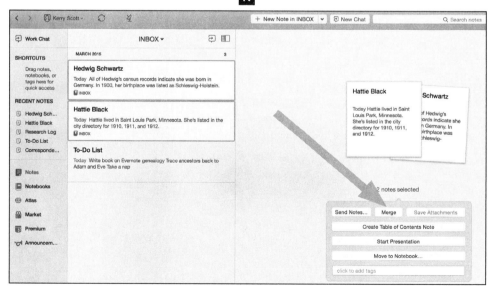

You can combine two notes into one using Evernote's Merge feature.

the item to the location where you want to include it. Dragging and dropping also works for moving notebooks around.

Deleting an Item

To delete a note, hover your mouse over it, right-click, then click Delete Note (image **M**). You also can click the trash can icon in the upper right corner of your note to delete it. The process for deleting notebooks and stacks is the same one used for deleting notes.

Merging Notes

Sometimes genealogists spend weeks (or months, or years) researching two different people, only to realize that they're actually the same person. If you've just figured out that Hedwig Schwartz and Hattie Black are one and the same, you'll probably want to merge the notes you've created about each of them. Doing this takes four simple steps:

1. Select as many notes as you need to merge by holding down the Control key (on Windows) or the Command key (on a Mac), then clicking each note.

2. You'll see a dialog box (image **N**) that gives you several options. Choose Merge.

3. Evernote will auto-select a title for your new note. To change it, just highlight the note title, then type over it.

4. Your old, individual notes will be moved to the Trash notebook, but all of the content will appear in your new, merged note.

KEYS to SUCCESS

✳ Think of Evernote's basic structure like a family: Notes are the main characters. They're where you'll spend the most time and energy. Notebooks hold notes. They're the parents of the main characters. Stacks hold notebooks. They're the grandparents of the main characters.

✳ Take advantage of Evernote's infinite organization possibilities to set up a system that's best suited to your genealogy needs. Options include sorting by document type, by branch of the family, and by the project you're working on.

✳ Keep organized with Evernote's additional tools, including shortcuts, recent notes lists, reminders, and to-do lists.

✳ Choose the Evernote screen view that makes the most sense to you. You aren't locked into the default view that you see on your screen, so experiment to determine what works best for your individual needs.

✳ Change up your notes as needed. You can move a note to a different notebook or stack, delete a note (or restore it from the trash), and merge multiple notes into one.

EVERNOTE ORGANIZATION WORKSHEET

Think about how you want to organize your notes within Evernote. Use this worksheet to sketch out ideas for your organization scheme. For items that don't fit into obvious categories, you may find it helpful to jot down potential notes first, then look for common themes to group them into notebooks or stacks.

My Evernote Organizing Scheme

Stacks	Notebooks	Sample Notes

Finding Data in Evernote

I'm going to let you in on two secrets for using Evernote that will help you become a better genealogist. The first is to use Evernote regularly so all of your important information is in one place. The second is to master Evernote's search capabilities so you can always find what you're looking for.

From your online genealogy research, you're probably used to long, complex search forms with many fields and options. Searching on Ancestry.com **<www.ancestry.com>**, FamilySearch.org **<www.familysearch.org>**, and other popular genealogy websites can feel overwhelming at times because there are so many options. Not so with Evernote. Mastering Evernote's search feature is easy—in fact, in many cases, it's as simple as typing in a word or phrase and hitting Enter. Even more complex searches are fairly intuitive in Evernote. No need to remember wildcards, search operators, or any sophisticated search techniques. In this chapter, I'll introduce you to how the search function works and how to customize it to your needs.

KEEPING YOUR MATERIALS ORGANIZED

The most basic principle of organization is ease of retrieval—the whole point is to be able to find what you want again. One way to ensure you can locate materials easily is to arrange them within a defined organizational structure so you don't have to go searching too hard for them. In genealogy, that often means filing data and documents by the name of a person (or possibly a place). Several factors can complicate the approach of organizing by name, though:

- Sometimes people change their names.
- Sometimes you don't yet know an ancestor's name (or how that name was spelled).
- Sometimes you haven't learned all the names an ancestor used yet (this happens frequently with women who had multiple spouses).

In these instances, tagging notes can be a lifesaver. Suppose you have a document that refers to Sara Graham. You put that document into Evernote as a note (or part of a note). When you search for that document, the only way you'll find it is by looking for Sara Graham—the name specifically listed on the document. But if you know that Sara was also known as Sara Hutchison, Sara Smith, and Sara Johnston, you can tag that original document with her other surnames, making them instantly searchable. Those additional surname tags will allow you to find the document no matter which of Sara's surnames you search on, even though those other names aren't listed anywhere on the document itself. You'll learn more about using tags in chapter 5.

Another important factor in keeping your notes organized is syncing your work to multiple devices. If you have Evernote installed on your desktop computer alone, you won't have the option of adding notes on the fly. This means you might be tempted to take notes on whatever's available—including a scrap of paper, a napkin, or a different app on your smartphone. This is why it's important to install Evernote on every device you can. If you have it everywhere, your notes will all end up in the right place, and you can't lose them, misplace them, or spill coffee on them. Just having Evernote with you at all times makes a big difference in staying organized and cuts down on your need to search for things.

When you're actually working with your notes, Evernote provides different ways to view them so you can find what you're looking for. You can sort your notes by any of the following:

- Title
- Date Created
- Date Updated
- Date Deleted (this is an option only in the trash folder, but it's superhelpful if you're looking for something you accidentally deleted within a particular time frame)

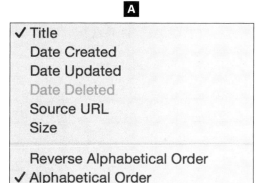

You can choose from a number of options when deciding how to sort a list of notes.

- Source URL (helpful for finding all of your notes from a particular website)
- Size

You can also choose to search in alphabetical (A–Z) or reverse alphabetical (Z–A) order. Follow these steps to change your sort order:

1. Open the notebook where you want to see your notes.

2. Choose View from the top menu, then choose Sort By in the drop-down menu.

3. A new menu with a list of sort options will appear (image **A**). Click the one you want, and your notes will appear in that order automatically.

Sorting is a quick but powerful tactic to find what you need. For example, maybe you want to review the notes you made while researching at your ancestors' county courthouse last summer. Sort by date created to group all those notes together, regardless of which notebooks they might live in. Or perhaps you'd like to browse through all the obituaries you clipped from GenealogyBank **<www.genealogybank.com>**. Sort by Source URL to pull them up instantly.

SEARCH BASICS

Even if you have the most organized notes possible, there will be times when it's faster and easier to just search for what you need. Evernote's simple, elegant search feature works in seconds. When you use it, keep in mind that your membership level affects what data Evernote will search:

- If you're a Basic user, you're searching the text of your notes, your tags, and any text that appears in photos (like a photo of an obituary or death certificate).

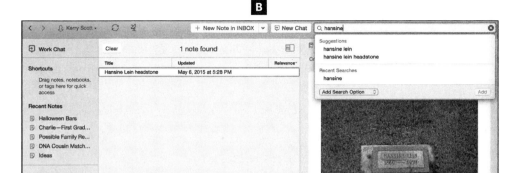

Searching for *Hansine* in my Evernote file brings up the one note that contains this name, plus a photo of the headstone. Evernote can read the text on the headstone, as well as the text in the note. Storing your headstone photos in Evernote is a great way to index them without any effort on your part.

- If you're a Plus subscriber, you're searching your text, your tags, and the text in your photos, plus the text of any e-mails you've sent to your special Evernote e-mail address.
- If you're a Premium subscriber, you're searching all of the above, plus the text of any PDFs you're storing in Evernote.

Conducting a Simple Search

You'll be able to find most notes by using the built-in search feature without any additional effort on your part. Conducting a basic search in Evernote can be done in four steps:

1. Navigate to the top search bar. It's next to the magnifying glass icon.

2. Type in the search term you want to use. The search isn't case sensitive—no need to capitalize any words you want to search on.

3. As you type, search results will appear. You'll see a list of Suggestions, which is Evernote's version of auto-completing your search term. For example, when I type in *Hansine* (image **B**), Evernote guesses that I'm looking for Hansine

POWER-USER TIP

Unrestricting Searches

If your search isn't bringing the expected result, don't panic. The most likely explanation is that you've accidentally enabled restricted searching. To fix this, click on the tiny drop-down arrow next to the magnifying glass in the search box, then click Search All Notes and try your search again.

Lein (who, as it happens, is the only Hansine in my notes). When Evernote finds multiple matches, you'll get more suggestions (image 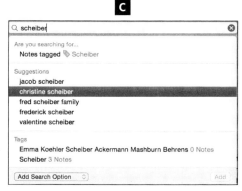). Click on the suggested text that matches what you're looking for, or keep typing if you want to narrow your results further.

4. You'll also see a list of recent searches, in case you want to repeat a search you've already done. If the recent searches list includes what you're looking for, click the search term to execute the search.

Adding Search Criteria

As your Evernote data grow, you may find that you have so many notes containing a particular name or location that you need to narrow your search criteria in order to find what you're looking for. Clicking the Add Search Option button at the bottom of your search box (image 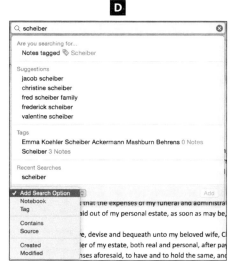) will allow you to narrow your search by one of the following criteria:

- Notebook
- Tag
- Contains (items contained in what you're searching for, such as pictures or audio; see box for the specific parameters you can define)
- Source (see box for the specific parameters you can define)
- Created (the date the note was created)
- Modified (the date the note was last changed)

C

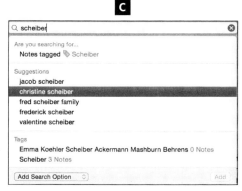

Searching for *Scheiber* brings up a number of notes, since that's a key name in my family. In this case, Evernote gives me several Scheibers to choose from under Suggestions, and it also allows me to choose to see only notes that are actually tagged "Scheiber."

D

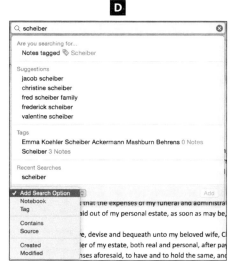

Click Add Search Option to see a menu of ways to narrow your search.

Keep Your Options Open

When you choose Contains or Source from the Add Search Options menu, you can pick from additional ways to refine your search. This crib sheet outlines your options.

Contains Options	Source options
audio files	e-mail
encryption	web page
images	mobile
to-do	desktop
completed to-dos	ScanSnap scanner
incomplete to-dos	
Moleskine notes	
Post-it Notes	

Saving a Search

If you conduct a particular search fairly frequently, you may want to consider saving it. For example, suppose you frequently need to find all headstones that are tagged #PleasantViewCemetery and have the surname Pumpernickel. To do that, you'll be using the tools outlined in the Adding Search Criteria section above. Re-creating those selections would be a hassle, but luckily you don't have to—Evernote lets you save up to one hundred searches. Here's how to set up a saved search:

1. Conduct your search using the criteria you need. Use the Add Search Option button to narrow your search as needed.

2. From your top menu, select Edit, then Find, then Save Search.

3. Type in the name you want to use for your saved search, then hit Enter.

You'll now see your saved search as an option whenever you perform searches. It will appear under Recent Searches. If you'd like to edit or delete your saved search, choose the Edit button next to the name of the search itself. You'll see the option to make changes or delete the saved search altogether.

Using Paper Notes

You might have noticed that your search options include paper notes in the form of Moleskine and Post-it Notes. But Evernote is electronic—so what gives? Those companies' products easily integrate with Evernote: Simply capture your paper scribblings to Evernote. The Moleskine Evernote Smart Notebook **<www.moleskine.com/us/news/evernote-smart-notebo-1>** even includes Smart Stickers that automatically become searchable tags after import. Find ideas for using Post-it notes with Evernote at **<www.post-it.com/wps/portal/3M/en_US/PostItNA/Home/Ideas/Evernote>**.

A WORD ABOUT SIMULTANEOUS SEARCH AND CONTEXT

If you've been an Evernote user for a while, you may have used (or at least heard of) Simultaneous Search. This tool was available to paid subscribers, and it allowed you to search Google, Yahoo!, or Bing at the same time you were searching your own notes.

This function has been replaced by a feature called Context. Now Premium subscribers have an automated tool that searches for information on the Web. For example, if you search your Evernote files for *notes on AncestryDNA*, it will show your notes from the webinar you attended or the cousin matches you've corresponded with. It will also pull up a recent article from *The Wall Street Journal* that talks about AncestryDNA.

This feature can be useful, but if you'd rather not use it, you can turn the Context function off in your Preferences settings.

KEYS to SUCCESS

✳ Minimize your need to search for items in Evernote by choosing an organizational structure that makes sense for your individual needs.

✳ Use tags and keywords in your notes to make it easier to find what you need later. Make use of Evernote's sorting options, too.

✳ Remember that your subscription level will determine how much of your material is searchable. Text in photos and PDFs are searchable only with paid memberships.

✳ If your search brings up too many results, add search criteria to help narrow it down.

EVERNOTE SEARCH CHECKLIST

Need to find an item in Evernote? Follow these steps to locate anything in a jiffy:

☐ Make sure you've synced Evernote across all your devices so all your data are up-to-date and available on the platform you're currently using.

☐ Start by entering a simple keyword search in the search bar.

☐ Review the recent searches that pop up; select one if it applies to what you're looking for.

☐ Add more search options if you get too many results.

☐ Use applicable sorting options to view like notes together.

☐ Save searches you expect to execute frequently.

Searches I Want to Save

_____

_____

_____

_____

_____

_____

_____

_____

_____

_____

_____

_____

Taking Advantage of Tags

In addition to titles and text, Evernote notes include another essential component for genealogists: tags. These are additional descriptive labels you create for your notes, and they're one of the most underrated tools in Evernote. People usually think of tags as a way to find an item or thought again, especially if you've seen or used them in other applications, such as for organizing photos or viewing related blog posts. But that's just the tip of the iceberg in terms of tags' usefulness.

For genealogists, tags are actually a powerful tool for analyzing your data. Family historians are constantly looking for ways to more effectively spot patterns, hidden clues, and easily overlooked connections between people, places, and things. Tags are the key to accomplishing this. In this chapter, we'll explore how to make the most of this secret weapon to enhance your genealogy research.

TAGGING BASICS

Before you can unleash the power of tags on your brick walls, you'll need to master the art of creating, modifying, and sorting them. Let's walk through the basics of tagging.

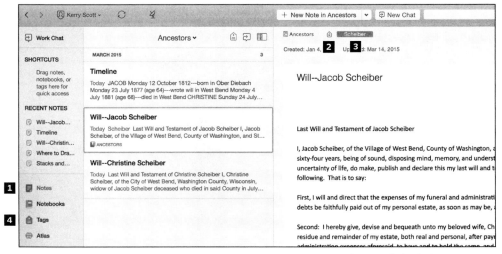

For a note containing the text of my ancestor Jacob Scheiber's will, I created a tag called *Scheiber*.

Creating a Tag

Creating a tag couldn't be easier. In fact, the process is so easy that it's tempting to create a plethora of tags for everything. Resist that temptation, because it's a gateway drug to ending up with so many tags that you'll never remember them all. Evernote allows you to have up to one hundred tags per note, but that's probably about ninety-five too many for most people.

To create tags, follow the steps below and labeled on image **A** for reference.

1. Open the note you wish to tag (or a brand-new note if you'd like). Here I've pulled up an existing note containing the will of Jacob Scheiber.

2. Navigate to the little tag icon at the top of your notes screen.

3. Type in the name of the tag you want. In this case, I'm creating a tag for a surname, so I've typed *Scheiber*. There's one quirk to tag names: They can't contain commas. Instead, Evernote converts commas to dashes. For genealogists, that means place-name tags will look a little weird. If you try to type *Carrington, North Dakota*, for example, your tag will actually show up as Carrington—North Dakota. It's a little irksome at first, but you won't even notice once you get used to it.

4. You also can create tags without notes. First, click on the Tags link on the left side of the Evernote screen, then click the New Tag button at the top. If you want to set up your tag structure before you begin making notes, this is the way to go.

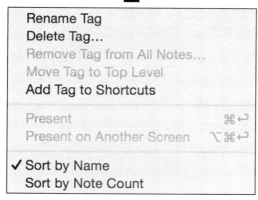

Right-click to see your tag editing options.

Editing Tags

Sooner or later, you'll need to edit one or more of your tags. Fortunately, that's easy to do:

1. Click on the Tags link in the left navigation menu.

2. Hover your mouse over the tag you want to work with, and right-click (control-click on Macs). A new menu will appear (image).

3. Choose Rename Tag to create a new name for your existing tag (without losing the notes it's attached to). Choose Delete Tag to remove the tag altogether.

Tagging Tools and Tips

Tags are highly flexible. You can arrange them in a variety of ways to ensure they're manageable, not overwhelming. These best practices will help you get the most out of tags.

- If you put a period at the beginning of your tag name, it will appear at the top of your list of tags (which, by default, is sorted alphabetically). This is handy if you want to make a particular tag stand out. Tags that start with numbers will appear after the ones with a period at the beginning, followed by tags starting with letters.

- The number displayed on the right side of a tag tells you how many items are linked to that particular tag. If you would like to sort your list of tags by the number of linked items

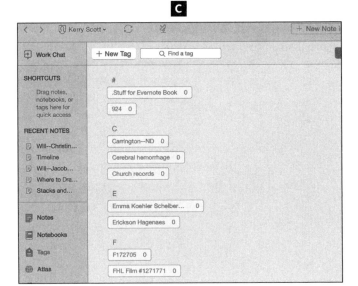

You have lots of options for keeping your tags organized so they're useful.

(most items to least items), click Note Count at the top of the Tags screen. This will change the order from alphabetical to the number of notes per tag, in descending order (image 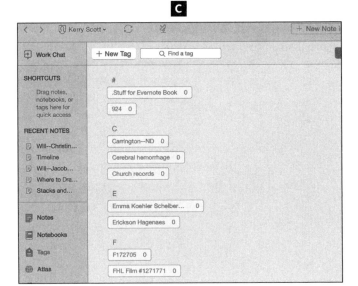).

- You can create "sub-tags" that nest under their parent tag. For example, you might have a tag called Research Trips, with sub-tags for your state historical society library, the town where a group of your ancestors came from, the Family History Library in Salt Lake City, and so forth.

- Evernote's limit for tags is one hundred per note, and one hundred thousand tags per Evernote account. Remember, though, that less is more. If you actually had one hundred thousand tags in use, it's unlikely that they'd do anything but bog you down and make you cranky.

USING TAGS TO DO BETTER RESEARCH

Tags are a great tool for organizing your notes, but they're even better at serving as a personal assistant. Few of us can remember every genealogy clue we've ever found, or instantly see the connection between a document we located in 1998 and another resource we used today. Evernote tags can serve as the backup brainpower you need to bridge those gaps. Let's take a look at some of the ways you can use tags for genealogical research.

Making Sense of Confusing Names

Wouldn't it be nice if our ancestors had made it easier for us to track them? In a perfect world, all our ancestors would have had rare names that are easy to search, spelled their monikers the same way every time, and never changed their names. Unfortunately, few of us descend from such considerate people—name complications constantly trip us up. But tags can make a number of name situations easier to manage. Let's look at several different scenarios.

PATRONYMS

Historically, a number of cultures used patronyms (some still use them even today). In the patronymic naming system, your "surname" (such as it is) is based on your father's first name. For example, suppose Lars Erickson has a son, Nels. Nels' surname is Larson, because his father's first name was Lars. When Nels Larson has a son named Ole, he's called Ole Nelson, because his father's first name was Nels. This goes on for generations, and it's the direct cause of many genealogists' gray hair. You can use tags to connect Ole Nelson, Nels Larson, and Lars Erickson. You might choose a tag such as Grandpa Ole's Line or Tysfjord Norwegians to distinguish them from your other people.

FARM NAMES

In some cultures, the patronym system is supplemented by a farm name. Lars Erickson comes from a farm in Norway called Hagenaes, so he's known as Lars Erickson Hagenaes. His son Nels is known as Nels Larson Hagenaes, and Ole is called Ole Nelson Hagenaes. This worked fine in the old country, but once these people arrived in the United

Don't Go Tag Wild

Caution: Tags are addictive. Many software programs offer tags to help you find data on your computer that might otherwise be lost. Because Evernote has such a robust search feature, though, you don't necessarily need a tag just to find something. Resist the urge to tag notes with words that already appear in the text of the note. If you're working with notes on your Jorgenson line, for example, you probably have the word Jorgenson in the document itself. Evernote will easily find those Jorgenson notes when you search, so you don't need an additional tag called Jorgenson to keep them from getting lost. You might, however, want to tag those Jorgensons with their farm name back in Norway, to distinguish the Jorgenson Viste family from the Jorgenson Fergum family. Tags are best used for cross-referencing, grouping things together, and analyzing clues—not for duplicating pre-existing search terms.

States, things got wacky. Ole might have chosen to be known as Ole Nelson in America, but his brother Arne may have decided to drop the patronym and go by Arne Hagenaes. Arne's son Erik, who was born in the United States and wanted to sound more American, may have dropped Hagenaes and gone by Erik Ness. Better still, many of these folks changed their mind a few times, so you might find them in different records under different names.

Shaking your fist in fury at these ancestors won't help, because they're dead. Tags, on the other hand, can connect all of these people to the right records. In fact, you can make a tag for this family and use it to label people you suspect may belong to them. That way, when you find Sigrid Hagen or Jens Ness, you can locate your related notes easily as you begin to explore whether they actually belong to this tough-to-trace line. Tags are great for making sure you don't forget about the "maybe-mine-maybe-not" people you find along the way.

Guide to Patronymic Suffixes in Scandinavia

Norway, Sweden, and Denmark are perhaps best known for their patronymic naming systems. While patronyms give you valuable clues to a father's name, a surname that changes with every generation can make it hard to trace a family over time. The "rules" for creating a patronym also changed with the time, place, and family.

As this chart from *Family Tree Magazine* illustrates, each Scandinavian country's residents used slightly different suffixes to form their patronymic surnames. Norway generally followed the pattern of the ruling country.

The chart holds true through most of the 1700s and 1800s. Then, as countries began passing laws that mandated fixed surnames, families slowly began adopting them. Late in the nineteenth century, many families, especially in Denmark, began using the male extension for both sons and daughters.

Country	Son	Daughter
Denmark	–sen	–datter
Sweden	–son	–dotter
Norway before 1814 (Danish rule)	–sen	–datter
Norway 1814–1905 (Swedish rule)	–son	–dotter
Norway after 1905 (independence)	–søn	–dotter

This enormous probate file contained my Emma under several of her various surnames. I tagged each page that related to her so they'd all come up together when I searched. This way, I'm sure I have everything I need when I'm working on research related to her, and there's no danger of confusing her with a different Emma.

MULTIPLE SURNAMES

Every genealogist has at least one Emma. She's that ancestor who got married over and over again and changed her name each time. You might not even know yet what all of her surnames will be, so it's hard to know what to file her under. It's even harder to spot her in records because you might not know all of the husbands' names yet.

My Emma started life as Emma Koehler. Her father died shortly before she was born, and her mother remarried when she was a baby. That made her Emma Scheiber. Then she got married and became Emma Ackermann. Mr. Ackermann seems to have run off to Europe, and when he finally died, Emma remarried and became Emma Mashburn. Mr. Mashburn was, well, not a keeper, as it turns out. So one divorce record and another marriage record later, she was Emma Behrens. Mr. Behrens lasted two decades, which proves that the third time really is the charm.

Emma Koehler Scheiber Ackermann Mashburn Behrens was one of the first ancestors I ever researched, and it took me years to unravel her story. I frequently overlooked her in records (such as the probate file in image **D**) because I didn't know what name to look for.

As a result, she was often staring me in the face with a name I didn't recognize. I missed clues in my research that would have helped me connect the dots much sooner. Using a tag named Emma in Evernote would have allowed me to pull *all* the Emma stuff connected with the rest of her family, and I would have had a much more useful timeline of her many surname changes that correspond to the records she left. (To this day, Emma is labeled simply "Emma" in my files. Like Madonna. I figure she earned it.)

Using Locations as Tags

Locations have always been important in genealogical research. Knowing a suspected ancestor came from a particular town or county can help you determine if he belongs in your family tree. Because records are kept and filed by location (in the United States, at the county, state, or federal level)—the place your ancestor resided guides where you'll look for records. As DNA testing has become more popular, location research is even more important. When your DNA test produces a daunting list of cousins with surnames you don't recognize, finding locations in common can be the key to figuring out how you're related. Let's look at several helpful applications for using location-related tags in Evernote.

LOCATION NAME CHANGES

Most veteran genealogists have had this experience: You look for records in a particular county where your ancestor lived. They're not there, but you find them (eventually) in a neighboring county. A generation before, you can't find the records—because they're in another county. Did your ancestors move? No. The county lines did.

Whether you're researching in the United States or internationally, you'll find that towns, states, provinces, and even entire countries have changed their names (or borders) repeatedly since your ancestors left records. You can ensure that you find *all* of the records from one place in your Evernote file (even when the location name doesn't match) by linking them with a common tag.

For example, if you're working with a family from Herkimer County, New York, you'll need to know that Herkimer County used to be part of Montgomery County, and that Onondaga, Chenango, and Oneida Counties were carved out of Herkimer County. Tagging records about your family with each of those county names (or with a common tag such as Upstate New York Lines) will help ensure that you don't miss any related items when you're working on them. If you applied that Upstate New York Lines tag to the *History of Herkimer County* book (image **E**), for instance, you wouldn't have to remember that Herkimer's parent county was Montgomery—you'd have the book and the answer at your fingertips through the power of tagging.

HISTORY OF HERKIMER COUNTY,

INCLUDING

THE UPPER MOHAWK VALLEY,

FROM THE

EARLIEST PERIOD TO THE PRESENT TIME:

WITH A

BRIEF NOTICE OF THE IROQUOIS INDIANS, THE EARLY GERMAN TRIBES,
THE PALATINE IMMIGRATIONS INTO THE COLONY OF NEW YORK,
AND BIOGRAPHICAL SKETCHES OF THE PALATINE FAMILIES,
THE PATENTEES OF BURNETSFIELD IN THE YEAR 1725.

ALSO

BIOGRAPHICAL NOTICES OF THE MOST PROMINENT
PUBLIC MEN OF THE COUNTY:

WITH

IMPORTANT STATISTICAL INFORMATION.

BY NATHANIEL S. BENTON.

ALBANY:
J. MUNSELL, 78 STATE STREET.
1856.

Tracking location name changes is important when you need to know what county history books to consult to find your family.

This mysterious photographer's stamp drove me crazy for decades. Thanks to Evernote's tagging, when another clue from Carrington, North Dakota, finally surfaced, I saw the connection immediately.

PLACES YOUR ANCESTORS VISITED

My second great-grandfather Frank Scheiber was the head of a family that moved all over the upper Midwest. I've painstakingly documented each of the locations they lived in, and I know one place they never lived: Carrington, North Dakota. Imagine my surprise when I inherited photos of Frank and his family and found one that had a photographer's stamp—from Carrington, North Dakota (image **F**). What was the connection to this town?

I had no idea then, but I tagged that photo *Carrington, North Dakota*, in Evernote in the hope of figuring it out. Years went by, and I forgot about the Carrington connection. Then I found another clue—a one-line newspaper account that said another relative had returned from a trip to Carrington. Over the years, I found a few more North Dakota clues and tagged them all, hoping it would pay off down the road.

More years went by, and I forgot about it again—until recently. In April 2015, I heard from a cousin on the Scheiber line, and he told me he remembered the old aunts traveling by train from Minnesota to California to visit his branch of the family. He recalled that they used to stop on the way back—in North Dakota. I pulled all of the records tagged with this location, and now, twenty years after the initial clue, I've finally figured out the North Dakota connection. Without Evernote, it's highly unlikely that I would have remembered each of those tiny clues over such as long span of time, and it's even less likely that I could have quickly found them, laid them out, and looked to see what they had in common. My Evernote tag allowed me to do that in a single click.

House numbers are another clue worth tagging. They can help you tie families together via census records, city directories, and land records.

Be ready for your next trip to the Family History Library in Salt Lake City by tagging items that require research there.

A word of caution: It's not necessarily productive to tag *every* location. But the ones that don't make sense or seem to come out of left field? Those are the ones that need a tag. Let the tags do the work of making those connections over time and space to help you see how they fit together.

HOUSE NUMBERS

Have you ever gotten out your magnifying glass and tried to pick out the house number in an old photo? Once you think you have it, scan that photo into Evernote, and tag it with the house number. Then tag your other photos that appear to be taken at the same house (image 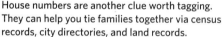). Now pull census records, city directories, and other records that include the same address and tag them with the house number.

Voilà! You now have a way to pull all these records together with a single click. That house number tag will let you compare records of the occupants with people who appear in the photos. That's an incredible tool for helping date those photos and determine the possible identities of the people pictured: If you have a photo of a house at 727 Apple Street that looks like it was taken around 1900, and a census record from 1900 that lists the people who lived there, you are well on your way to identifying every person in that photo.

RESEARCH TRIPS AND REPOSITORIES

Few of us can afford to take all of the research trips we'd like to. When we do have the opportunity to visit a location or repository that might have information we need, we usually need to make the most of every minute of our time there. One way to make trip planning easier and maximize efficiency while working on site is to use tags to label things we need to do.

For example, if you're working on a family from Bernalillo County, New Mexico, you might like to pull the probate file for your ancestor when you visit the county courthouse. Your visit there might be years away, though, so you can tag your notes with this location. Then, three months from now, you might be researching something else and find you have another record housed in Bernalillo County. Over time, you'll build up an inventory of tags related to that location.

When you've finally saved up enough money and/or convinced your spouse to vacation in New Mexico, you'll just need to pull up the Bernalillo County tag to see exactly what you need to work on during your visit. You won't have to spend time scrambling around making a list, and you'll be able to use that time buying sunscreen (and if you're visiting New Mexico, you'll need it).

You can use this tagging tactic for specific repositories, not just locations. Nearly every genealogist has a wish list for a trip to the Church of Jesus Christ of Latter-day Saints' Family History Library in Salt Lake City **<www.familysearch.org/locations/saltlakecity-library>** (image **H**), so a tag called SLC—FHL is a good one to have. You could even use this for local research destinations, such as your local library, courthouse, or vital-records office. If you happen to be running errands nearby, you can stop in and the list of records you need will be right at your fingertips.

SCHOOLS

Many of us research ancestors for years (or even decades) without ever seeing a photo of them. For relatives you've come to "know" through your hard work, there's nothing more satisfying than finding a photo that shows you what they actually looked like. Yearbooks (image **I**) are one way you can finally lay your hands on a picture of your

---

This tattered 1933 yearbook from West High School in Minneapolis is one of my prized possessions. I bought it on eBay, and when it arrived, I learned that my grandpa was a member of the History Club in high school. That's a family trait I never would have known about otherwise.

ancestor, but yearbooks are not always easy to come by. Subscription-based websites such as Ancestry.com <www.ancestry.com> and E-Yearbook.com <www.e-yearbook.com> make digital copies of yearbooks available to subscribers, but their collections are hit or miss. Auction websites such as eBay <www.ebay.com>, though, can be a great resource for yearbooks. The challenge: When you need a particular volume, it's often not for sale, and when a particular volume is available, it's hard to quickly scan your entire database to see whether that volume might include an ancestor.

By tagging ancestors with the name of the school they would have attended and the year they would have graduated, you can have that information at your fingertips. Set up

Visiting a FamilySearch Center

Did you know you can access the Family History Library's microfilmed genealogical records without going to Salt Lake City? FamilySearch, the genealogy arm of the Church of Jesus Christ of Latter-day Saints, makes those resources available to rent through a network of local FamilySearch Centers. With forty-six hundred centers around the world, chances are good there's one near you (find out at **<www.familysearch.org/locations>**).

When planning to visit a FamilySearch Center, heed these tips from *Family Tree Magazine*:

- **Call ahead for updated hours, especially if you're visiting a small center.** It doesn't hurt to call again the day of your visit to be sure the center is open. Centers are volunteer-staffed, so if the person who's supposed to open that day is sick or stuck at home in bad weather, there might not be a backup person waiting to fill in.

- **Have an idea of the records you're looking for.** Your best bet is to search the FamilySearch Catalog **<www.familysearch.org/catalog-search>** and order microfilm online in advance. Keep tabs on your microfilm needs and orders in Evernote—you might use a tag such as Norwood Ohio FamilySearch Center or My Local FamilySearch Center.

- **One microfilm often leads to another, so you may need to order more films for later viewing.** Bring cash with you if you plan to rent film or make copies at the center. Film rental fees are due when you place the order, and most centers can't take checks or credit. It takes about four to six weeks for a microfilm to arrive.

For more details on Family History Centers, and links to information about specific centers (where available), see the FamilySearch Wiki **<www.familysearch.org/learn/wiki/en/Introduction_to_LDS_Family_History_Centers >**.

a search on eBay for yearbooks from the schools near where your ancestors lived (eBay calls this "following" a search—find instructions and tips at **<pages.ebay.com/help/buy/searches-follow.html>**). It might be years before you get a hit, but when you do, you can quickly search your tags to see if that particular volume is going to be one you'll want. If it is, start the bidding. If not, you know you haven't missed out on something you actually needed.

More Uses for Tags

Locations and names are fairly straightforward uses for tags, but there are some other, less obvious ways that tags can make your genealogical life easier. Next, we'll dive into a sampling of such creative uses of tagging for family history research.

RECORD TYPES

Tagging records by type helps you pull up all of the birth records or wills in your collection. This is particularly handy if you're trying to decipher one record and need an easier-to-read version from the same time or place to help you make sense of it. If you do any genealogical writing or lecturing, it's helpful to have examples of specific types of genealogical documents at the ready.

Additionally, you can prioritize your record ordering (and your related budget) by looking at a similar record to determine if it will have the information you need. If you're contemplating whether to order a Minnesota death record from 1903, for instance, it's helpful to know if such a record would list the names of the parents. (Spoiler alert: It would not. You just saved nine dollars.)

CAUSE OF DEATH AND MEDICAL INFORMATION

It's a well-known fact that some types of medical conditions run in families. If you're trying to determine if a particular ailment runs in your own family, tags can help you track that. Keep in mind that the names of various illnesses have changed over time, so you'll want to be consistent. For example, a stroke used to be called apoplexy, and epilepsy used to be known as the falling sickness—see The Cure for Confusing Disease Names for more. Be consistent, whether you use the old names or the current ones.

FAMILYSEARCH MICROFILM NUMBERS AND OTHER SOURCES

Even if you do most of your genealogical research online, you're bound to do at least a little of your legwork the old-fashioned way. After all, there's a plethora of records and resources in archives, libraries, and other repositories that haven't been digitized and posted online (at least not yet). Ordering microfilm, waiting for it to arrive, then loading it onto a reader is still a way of life for many genealogists. Sound familiar? If so, you are already familiar with those FamilySearch microfilm numbers that identify each reel of microfilm from the massive global records collection of the Family History Library. (If you're new to FamilySearch microfilms, see the Visiting a FamilySearch Center sidebar.)

When you order a new FamilySearch microfilm to view at your local Family History Center, tag your notes from the resulting research with that film number. Make notes on not only the content, but also the quality of the film, any quirks or irregularities and other characteristics you might need to know if you work with this film again. You might need to go back and revisit these records at some point in the future, and it will be helpful to be able to refresh your memory about what you're in for. If your notes tell you the film was so faint it was nearly unreadable, that will prompt you to seek out a different copy of the record, which will save you time and money.

The Cure for Confusing Disease Names

Flummoxed by an old cause of death or disease? This chart from the *Family Tree Pocket Reference*, second edition (Family Tree Books, 2013), demystifies bygone terminology for some common ailments. Find more archaic medical terms at **<www.antiquusmorbus.com>**.

Old Name	Modern Name
ablepsia	blindness
acute angina	sore throat
apoplexy	paralyzed by stroke
bad blood	syphilis
biliousness	jaundice cause by liver disease
black death	typhus
bladder in throat	diphtheria or whooping cough
brain fever	meningitis
caduceus	epilepsy
camp or ship's fever	typhus
catarrhal	cold or allergies
child bed fever	infection following childbirth
chin cough	diphtheria or whooping cough
cholelithiasis	gallstones
congestive fever or chills	malaria
consumption (also African consumption or galloping consumption)	tuberculosis
coryza	cold or allergies
costiveness	constipation
croup	laryngitis, diphtheria, or strep throat
dengue	infectious fever common in East Africa
dysentery	diarrhea
dyspepsia	heartburn, indigestion

Old Name	Modern Name
falling sickness	epilepsy
fatty liver	cirrhosis
fever n' ague	malarial fever
green sickness or fever	anemia
grippe, grip, or la grippe	influenza (the flu)
infantile paralysis	polio
keuchhusten	diphtheria or whooping cough
lues disease	syphilis
lumbago	lower back pain
lung or winter fever	pneumonia
lung sickness	consumption
malignant sore throat	diphtheria or whooping cough
mormal	gangrene
neuralgia	general term for discomfort (e.g. "neuralgia in the head" is a headache)
puerperal exhaustion	death due to childbirth
pox, French or great	syphilis
putrid fever	diphtheria or whooping cough
quinsey	tonsillitis
screws	rheumatism
sugar diabetes	insulin-dependent (Type 1) diabetes
thrush or aphtha	childhood disease; spots on mouth, lips, and throat

This can be an effective technique for noting the idiosyncrasies of other sources as well, so you have them for future reference.

FRIENDS, ASSOCIATES, AND NEIGHBORS

In order to break down your most stubborn brick walls, you often have to branch out to research the people around your ancestors. Noted author and genealogist Elizabeth Shown Mills calls this the FAN approach (short for Friends, Associates, and Neighbors); it's also sometimes referred to as "cluster genealogy." Whatever you call this technique, it works. In order to be most effective, though, you'll need to carefully label these non-relatives in your genealogy files, so you don't wonder years later what these random strangers are doing in your notes. By tagging each "FAN" with the name of the ancestor she's associated with, you'll ensure that your FANs are connected to the right people and breaking down the right brick walls. You'll also more easily spot connections by tagging people you might find years apart.

DNA COUSINS

If you haven't been bitten by the DNA bug yet, your time is coming. DNA testing has opened up a whole new world of possibilities for genealogists, but it's also created an entirely new set of challenges when it comes to staying organized and analyzing results. You can use Evernote tags to label your notes about various cousin matches to help you spot clues to help you determine how you're related.

For those who aren't familiar with genetic genealogy, here's a quick overview: Genealogy DNA tests analyze specific genetic markers, which are compared with other test-takers' DNA to determine relationships and ethnic ancestry. Effectively, you're looking for other people who match on the same markers; you and your matches can then analyze your traditional genealogical research to figure out exactly how you're related. The nature of DNA testing is such that you might have a match in 2015, but you might not be able to figure out the common ancestor until you have another match in 2016 and another in 2017. For that reason, it's especially important to have a method of tracking clues over long periods of time, without relying on memory.

In Evernote, you can use tags to label matches by chromosome number (which chromosome the other person matches you on), by ethnicity (because your Hungarians and your Norwegians don't necessarily match each other), by location (because a match with connections to your ancestors' rural county of origin might be related to you on that same line), or even by GEDmatch kit number or AncestryDNA username. (AncestryDNA <www.dna.ancestry.com> is the genetic genealogy division of Ancestry.com; GEDmatch <gedmatch.com> is a helpful online tool for analyzing and comparing DNA test results.)

Figuring out how you're related to hundreds of brand-new cousins is a daunting task, but tags can help you spot the patterns that lead to connections.

As you can see, tags function a bit like bread crumbs. You can use them to find the trail to the right ancestor in the right place at the right time. Tags boost your own analytical power and help you keep track of small clues you may have forgotten.

KEYS to SUCCESS

* Understand that because of Evernote's powerful search feature, you don't need tags simply to find something. You *do* need tags to help see connections in your research that might not be obvious.

* Use tags sparingly to avoid becoming overwhelmed. You can add one hundred tags per note, but you shouldn't.

* Take advantage of tags' unique organizational structure. For example, a period at the start of a tag name will send it to the top of your list of tags. You can group like items together with sub-tags and tell how many notes are associated with each tag by looking at the count next to the tag name.

* Use tags to help you do faster, more effective research. Consider creating tags to make sense of names and places, plan for research outings, identify ancestors' associates, track DNA cousin matches—any grouping that will help you analyze your findings faster and more easily.

Using Different Types of Data

The beauty of Evernote is that it doesn't limit you to just one type of data. Genealogists collect a lot of "stuff," and Evernote works with all of it. In this chapter, we'll go over each type of content you might want to work with and discuss ways to use Evernote and its various features to streamline your genealogy work flow and get more work done in less time.

TEXT NOTES

Text notes are where most Evernote users start. When you open a new note, you'll type in a title and be ready to go. Your screen looks similar to a word processing or e-mail entry screen, and Evernote's note section functions in a similar way. Depending on which platform you're using, you'll have a number of familiar formatting options:

- font
- text size
- bold
- italics

You can create tables in notes to help you organize your data in Evernote.

- underline
- text color
- highlight

You also have the option of creating a table in a note, similar to the way you create a table in Microsoft Word. To create a table in a note, follow these steps (labeled for easy reference on image **A**):

1. Open your note and type in a title. Hit Enter to move down to the note entry area.

2. Choose the grid icon in the toolbar. Use your mouse to choose the size of the table you want.

3. Use the Table Properties link to create a larger table (more than six columns and/or six rows). In the resulting menu, you can also choose the thickness and color of the table border, change the alignment (left, center, or right), and alter the cell background color (which is white by default).

Hit Enter to create your table. You can use your mouse to drag the borders to change the column width to meet your needs. The row height will auto-adjust to accommodate the amount of text you enter in that row.

Tables have a variety of uses for genealogists. You can use them to create research and correspondence logs or forms for entering census data. We'll go over some real-life family history uses for tables in chapter 8.

POWER-USER TIP

Rethinking Tables

When you're creating a table in Evernote, you'll quickly discover that it's not like a spreadsheet. Although you can have a maximum width of thirty columns, the resulting table fields are too narrow to be of much use for many genealogical applications (such as census abstracts). The solution is to turn your census abstract on its side so the headers run down the right and the people go across the top. We'll explore this more in chapter 8.

B

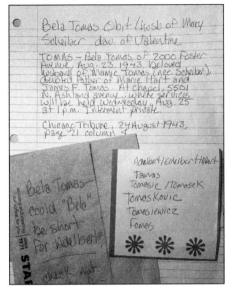

Most genealogists have a large collection of scraps of paper with information on them.

C

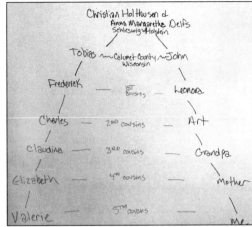

Hand-drawn trees illustrating what degree of relationship you have with a cousin can be captured in Evernote by taking a photo.

HANDWRITTEN NOTES

Nearly every genealogist has a pile of handwritten notes somewhere. In fact, many of us have notes written on napkins, paper towels, gum wrappers, and whatever else was available when inspiration struck or Uncle Felix started talking (image **B**). Even handwritten family trees, so important to a genealogist sifting through an ancestor's records, can be hard to keep track of (image **C**). It's challenging to organize handwritten notes, especially when they contain information about multiple ancestors. Which person should you file them under? How would you find them again? Would those gum wrappers get lost in your file cabinet?

As we've already discussed, Evernote can help you preserve these valuable resources. You can, of course, pull out each and every scrap and type it into Evernote as an individual note. But that's a tedious, time-consuming task, and you'll probably never get around to it. Instead, consider making use of another of Evernote's features by taking photos of your old notes.

There are several ways to get photos of your notes into Evernote, depending on what devices you use. Here we'll review the most likely candidates for getting the job done: digital camera and smartphone or tablet.

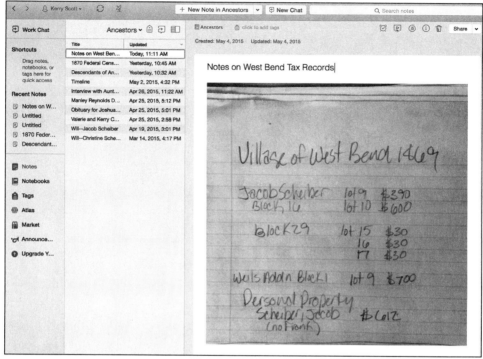

This photo of an old handwritten note was taken with a regular digital camera, then dragged into an Evernote note.

Taking Photos of Notes With a Digital Camera

It may come as a shock to some, but there are many happy, healthy twenty-first-century genealogists who don't use a smartphone or tablet. For those people, using a regular digital camera is a fine option for photographing notes. Here's how that works:

1. Take the photos you need. You can choose to photograph each note individually or put related notes together into one image. The latter approach works especially well if you're the type who has notes on countless tiny scraps of paper.

2. Transfer the photos you've taken to your computer, and make a note of the names and location of the corresponding files.

3. Open Finder (on a Mac) or File Explorer (on a PC), then open Evernote. This works best if you have both windows open at the same time, so you may need to make your windows smaller to fit them both on your screen simultaneously.

4. Drag the photo files into an open Evernote note (image). The note can be blank or already have content inside. You can add as many photos to a note as you'd like, but keep in mind your maximum note size (25MB for Basic users, 50MB for Plus users,

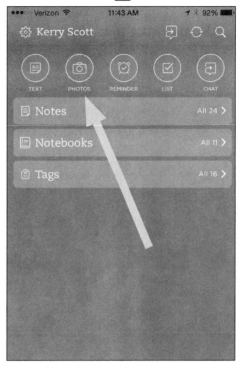

POWER-USER TIP

Have an Eye for Eyefi

If you're using a regular digital camera and have lots of notes to digitize, consider getting an EyeFi card for your camera. Your camera has a little SD card in it, and that's where your images are stored until you upload them to your computer. An EyeFi card is an SD card with a special superpower: It allows you to transfer your photos wirelessly. This means you no longer have to take all the photos, sit down at your computer, and manually upload them. Instead, while you're taking your photos, the ones you just took are beaming themselves to your computer. It's a huge timesaver for genealogists, who often have a large volume of papers to photograph and upload. You can find EyeFi cards at big box stores such as Target and Best Buy, or at online stores that sell electronics, such as Amazon.com. EyeFi cards are great for portable scanners like Doxie and Flip-Pal, too.

The Photos icon is one of the best Evernote features, allowing you to take pictures of notes, headstones, and even error messages on your computer.

and 200MB for Premium users). Photo files tend to be large, so check their size before you fill up a single note.

5. Type in whatever accompanying notes you like, and add tags as needed.

Taking Photos of Notes With Your Smartphone or Tablet

If you have a smartphone or tablet, the process of getting pictures into Evernote is even easier. Evernote has a built-in camera app that's separate from your device's regular camera, meaning your images won't end up in your camera roll (on iOS) or photo albums (on Android and other tablets). Instead, they'll go directly to Evernote. Here's how to use the camera app:

1. Open the Evernote app on your tablet or smartphone, then click the Camera icon (image **E**). It's the second icon from the left on the current version of the Evernote app.

2. Aim at the document you need to capture, allow the autofocus to operate for a second or two, then take the photo. Evernote has different options at the bottom—Post-it Note, Photo, Document, and Business Card—but for most genealogy-related applications, you'll see the best results on the Photo setting.

3. Once you've taken the photo, a checkmark appears in the lower right corner of the screen. Click it.

4. Click the link titled Snapshot at the top of the Notes list. The snapshot you took most recently will always be at the top of the list.

5. You'll see the photo you just took. Check to be sure it's readable, then type in whatever notes you would like and add tags as needed. Be sure to add a title to your note by clicking next to the word *Snapshot* at the top, then typing your preferred title over it. When you're done, click the elephant in the top left corner to go back to the main screen.

Another Option for Handwritten Notes

If you have a tablet, you have another way to add handwritten notes. Using an app called Penultimate and a stylus, you can actually write notes directly on your tablet. If you really want to eliminate paper, this is a great option (and it makes you look really cool at confer-

A Case Study in Clutter

Confession: I am the worst notetaker in the world. It's likely that a good 80 percent of my old genealogy notes are on something other than a normal piece of paper. In fact, my genealogical life began when I was a sophomore in high school and visited my grandmother shortly before she died. I was sitting at her kitchen table, and she began talking about my grandfather's family. I took notes on the only thing that was handy: a paper bag. I still have it. It even has the receipt from the snacks it once contained.

My pre-Evernote genealogy files contain notes written on sticky notes, napkins, paper towels, a candy bar wrapper, old envelopes, a page from my mortgage documents, and even a piece of toilet paper. The latter happened when a normally uncooperative relative mentioned a key piece of information about her grandmother, and I retreated to the bathroom to write it down before I forgot it. As a collector of nonstandard writing surfaces, I can tell you from experience: These notes won't last. The paper deteriorates, the ink fades, and your clues are lost. My notes only go back to the early 1990s, and some of them are already unreadable.

If you have a similar collection, put this book down and photograph those notes right now. Once they're gone, they're gone. Then repent (as I have) and keep your future notes in Evernote, where they aren't subject to the same ravages of time.

ences and genealogical society meetings). This also allows you to transcribe your collection of notes without having to use a type interface or rely on Evernote's camera to pick up your handwriting. We'll talk more about how to use Penultimate in chapter 10.

E-MAILS

It may seem hard to believe, but e-mail has been around for decades. This means that nearly every genealogist has a collection of e-mails that relate to family history. Whether you subscribe to newsletters, correspond with cousins, or write to repositories, it's highly likely that you have a number of old e-mail messages you need to keep. You'll want to be able to locate them easily, and you might want to tag them to cross-reference with the people, locations, or repositories they relate to.

Evernote was set up to meet this need from the beginning. Users who signed up for Evernote prior to May 2015 were assigned a unique e-mail address, and that address routed messages directly into their Evernote files. For example, if you signed up with the username SuperGenie, your assigned e-mail address might have been *supergenie5c0w7g9k@m.evernote.com*.

When Evernote introduced its current tiers of subscription plans, things changed. Now Plus and Premium users have the special e-mail address, but Basic users do not. It's important to understand, though, that Basic users had this special e-mail address prior to May 2015. That means you may run into old message forums or blog posts that give out this e-mail address. Whether it's active or not will depend on whether that person is a Plus or Premium subscriber in the particular month you're e-mailing in. It also means that if you go back and forth between free and paid subscriptions, your own special e-mail address will disappear and reappear.

It's easy to print an e-mail to PDF on a Mac.

Whether you're a Basic user or a Plus/Premium subscriber, there are ways to save e-mails to your Evernote file, but the process will be much simpler if you choose a paid account.

Saving E-mails for Basic Users

If a paid subscription just isn't in your budget, you still have some options in terms of saving important data from e-mails. How you'll handle this depends on the nature of the content in the e-mail.

PLAIN-TEXT CONTENT

If you're working with plain text (for example, a narrative that someone typed out), you might be able to simply copy and paste the text into an Evernote file. To do this, highlight the e-mail text using your mouse, then hit Control-C (on a PC) or Command-C (on a Mac). Open your Evernote note, then hit Control-V (on a PC) or Command-V (on a Mac). The text will appear, and you can reformat as needed.

FORMATTED CONTENT

If you're working with something fancier, such as a formatted newsletter from your local genealogical society, the copy-and-paste method will only create an unreadable mess. In that case, your best option is probably going to be to convert your e-mail to PDF, then save the PDF to Evernote. Here's how to do this:

- Open the e-mail, then use your e-mail client's Print option to format it for printing. This ensures that the printout will be in alignment and won't spill over the page.

- Use your operating system's print-to-PDF function to save the e-mail as a PDF. On a Mac, click Print, then click Change under the name of the destination printer (image **F**). Choose Save as PDF under Local Destinations. On a PC, depending on which version of Windows you use, you may need to download a free utility to do this (CutePDF **<www.cutepdf.com>** and PrintFriendly **<www.printfriendly.com>** are popular options among genealogists).

Keep in mind that if you're a Basic user, your PDF will not be searchable in Evernote. That means it's important to tag the PDF or type in some text notes with key details about the content to ensure that you can find it again when you need it.

Saving E-mails for Plus and Premium Subscribers

Saving e-mails is a much easier process when you're a paid Evernote subscriber. All you have to do is forward the e-mail to your special Evernote e-mail address, and it will appear in your Evernote file. To find your unique e-mail address, follow these steps:

1. Log in to your account through the web version of Evernote by navigating to **<www. evernote.com>**.

G

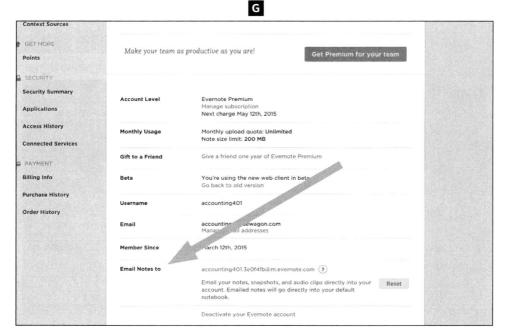

You can find your special Evernote e-mail address on the Account Summary page.

2. In the top left corner, click on Account.

3. A pop-up menu will appear. Click Settings.

4. You'll see a page called Account Summary (Image **G**). At the bottom, you'll see the Email Notes To section. That e-mail address is unique to your Evernote account, and anything sent there will end up in your default notebook. If you choose to share it, choose wisely so it doesn't end up a repository for spam.

Because e-mailed notes automatically go into your default notebook, you'll want to specify your default notebook so you know exactly where those e-mails end up. Many Evernote users set up a notebook called INBOX for this reason, then set that one as their default. The process works likes this:

1. Navigate to the Notebooks page by clicking on the Notebooks link in the left navigation menu.

2. Click the New Notebook button at the top of the screen. You'll be prompted to enter a name for your new notebook. Type INBOX (putting it in all caps makes it easier to spot when you have lots of notebooks).

3. Your new notebook will appear in the list of notebooks. Hover your mouse over it, then right-click (control-click on Macs). A pop-up menu will appear.

4. Choose Notebook Settings from the menu (image **H**). When the dialog box appears, choose "Make this my default notebook" and click Save (image **I**).

You can perform some special tricks when you actually forward your e-mail. Here are your options for being even more organized:

- Use the **@ symbol** in the subject line to send your e-mail to a specific notebook instead of your default INBOX. For example, when I receive e-mail newsletters from the Minnesota Genealogical Society **<www.mngs.org/mo_newsletter.php>**, I forward them with the subject line *@MGS Newsletters*. That puts them into the notebook I've created with that name.

- Use the **# symbol** in the subject line to tag your e-mail, using tags you have set up in Evernote. For example, if the Minnesota Genealogical Society newsletter has an especially good article on Frostbite Falls (home of my erstwhile Uncle Bullwinkle), I might add *#frostbitefalls #bullwinkle* to the subject line. The note containing this newsletter will be tagged automatically, so I'll easily find it the next time I work on this line (even if I'd forgotten I had the newsletter).

- Use **!Reminder** in the subject line to have Evernote's Reminder feature prompt you to act on this e-mail in the future. For example, if you receive an e-mail cousin from a new DNA match while you're on vacation, you're probably not going to be able to

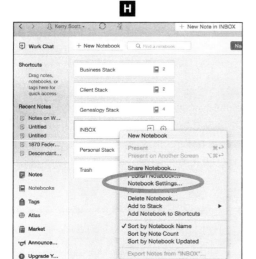

Go to Notebook Settings to make INBOX your default destination for incoming e-mails in Evernote.

Check "Make this my default notebook" to set each incoming e-mail to be deposited into this notebook.

work on figuring out your shared connection right away. You could leave it in your e-mail's inbox, but that leads to a cluttered inbox, and you might forget about it. Forward it to your Evernote file, and you'll be reminded to take action. If you want to be reminded on a specific date, you can put that in as well by adding another ! with the year/month/day, like this: *!Reminder !2016/03/31.*

You can use all of these tricks at the same time. For example, let's say I receive an e-mail message about a blog post I wrote about my husband's family. It relates to his Goeser line in Brothertown, Wisconsin. I'm busy writing this book, but I don't want to forget to get back to this person. I'll forward the e-mail to my special Evernote address, with the following subject line: *@In-Law Family #Brothertown #Calumet #Wisconsin #Goeser !Reminder !2015-11-16.* That means it'll go into the notebook I've designated for my husband's family, tagged with Brothertown (the town), Calumet (the county), and Wisconsin (the state). It also means that this reminder will come up after the book is finished, when I have time to work on it. This keeps my e-mail clean and ensures that I don't forget about this new lead.

There are so many exciting possibilities for using your Evernote e-mail address to be more organized and efficient. Just for starters, you could

- set up a rule in your e-mail program to auto-forward all of your genealogy newsletters. This keeps them all nice and neat in one place and gives you the opportunity to search for them. In fact, you could even subscribe to newsletters directly using your Evernote e-mail address, so they never clutter up your regular e-mail inbox.

- forward the myriad e-mails you receive once you've registered for a conference or event so you have them in the right notebook when you actually go to the conference. Your syllabus (in PDF form) can be stored in the same notebook so it's truly one-stop shopping for your conference experience.

- forward your airline and hotel confirmations for research trips to your Travel notebook so you have your itinerary and confirmation numbers all in one place. This is especially handy years later when you're trying to remember the name of that great hotel you stayed at the last time you did research in that location. I keep my notes on good restaurants, coffee shops, and other attractions in the same notebook so I have everything I need to plan a trip the next time.

Text Messaging and Genealogy

Not everyone loves e-mail. A growing number of people prefer the speed and brevity of text messaging. In fact, one development that's changed this landscape quite a bit is DNA testing. If you've worked with an adoptee or someone with unknown parentage, you know that the adrenaline runs high when you're close to finding the right person. You're finding clues at warp speed, and text messaging is a much better fit for this type of experience. My favorite cousin and I went through this when we were working on her adoption case, and as a result, I have a huge text messaging history with photos and important clues in it. I wanted to be sure to save that information—but how?

If you have an iOS device, you're in luck. There's a tool called iExplorer that allows you to export both iMessages (those from another iOS device) and SMS messages (those from a different platform). It even imports voicemail messages. Once they're exported, you can store the file in Evernote, where you'll be able to find it again. If you have a lot of text messages that need to be preserved, iExplorer **<www.macroplant.com/iexplorer>** is worth a look.

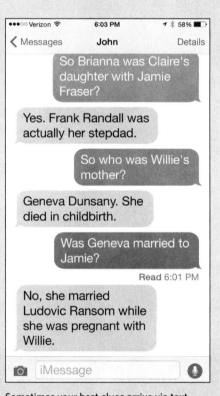

Sometimes your best clues arrive via text message.

- create a rule in your e-mail program that automatically forwards any e-mails from certain correspondents. Once you find a new cousin, you might be e-mailing back and forth with that person for years. You'll want to be sure to save all of that genealogy correspondence and to make it searchable, taggable, and easy to find. Storing those e-mails in Evernote is a great way to do that.

DOCUMENTS AND PHOTOGRAPHS

If there's one thing all genealogists have in common, it's a mountain of documents and family photos. From vital records to fat probate files to maps to newspaper clippings, the paper begins to pile up the minute you start researching your family history.

Evernote is ideal for storing all of your genealogy-related documents and pictures. You can tag them, annotate them, and even search the text contained within them. That means if you take a photo of an obituary and add it to an Evernote note, you will be able to search every word of that obituary. That's a game-changing superpower for any genealogist.

Capturing Your Documents and Photos With a Digital Camera

If you don't have a scanner or smartphone, a digital camera is going to be your best option for capturing your documents. In fact, even if you do have a scanner or smartphone, you might find that a camera is easier. It's generally faster than a scanner, and it's entirely possible that your image quality (particularly for documents) will be better than that of your smartphone. Here's how to capture documents with a camera and import them into Evernote:

1. Take an individual photo of each document or photograph. I've found that this works best for me when I work in batches of twenty or so, so that I can get into a rhythm without having too many files to work with at once.

2. Upload the photos you've taken and make a note of where the corresponding files end up.

3. Open your Finder (on a Mac) or File Explorer (on a PC), then open Evernote. This works best if you have both windows open at the same time, so you may need to make your windows smaller to fit them on your screen simultaneously.

4. Drag the document photo files into an open Evernote note. The note can be blank or already have content in it. You can do one photo per note or include several that relate to each other (like the birth, marriage, and death certificates for an individual ancestor or obituaries for the same person from multiple newspapers). Remember your maximum note size (25MB for Basic users, 50MB for Plus users, and 200MB

for Premium users). Photo files can be quite large, so check their size before you add too many to a single note.

5. Type in whatever accompanying notes you'd like and add tags as needed. Keep in mind that if you're dealing with printed text (like that of a newspaper clipping), Evernote will index each word, so you don't need to retype any of those words in order to find it again.

Capturing Photos and Documents With Your Smartphone or Tablet

The camera that's best for capturing photos or documents is often the one you have in your pocket. Since many of us carry our smartphones everywhere, these devices are almost always available, and that means we'll never miss an opportunity to record some exciting find. Evernote's built-in camera app is the ideal tool for capturing what you need because it saves you the step of actually adding them to Evernote (image ◼). Here's how to use it:

1. Open the Evernote app on your tablet or smartphone, then click the Camera icon. It's the second icon from the left on the current version of the Evernote app.

2. Aim at the document you need to capture, allow the autofocus to operate for a second or two, then take the photo. Evernote will automatically detect whether you're photographing a document or a photograph (as opposed to a sticky note or business card).

3. Once you've taken the photo, a checkmark appears in the lower right corner of the screen. Click it.

4. Click the link titled Snapshot at the top of the Notes list. The snapshot you took most recently will always be at the top of the list.

5. You'll see the photo you just took. Check to make sure the document is legible, then type in whatever notes you'd like and add tags as needed. Be sure to add a title to your note by clicking next to the word *Snapshot* at the top, then type your preferred title over it. When you're done, click the elephant in the top left corner to go back to the main screen.

Capturing Your Documents or Photos With a Scanner

If you don't have a steady hand, you can still scan your documents instead of taking pictures. These scanned images work similar to regular photographs, and you'll import them essentially the same way. Here's the process for importing your scanned papers:

1. Scan each document individually. I like to sort my documents in advance and scan them in batches that correspond to what notebooks I'll be adding them to.

> CHRYSANTH GOESER I
>
> BROTHER TO STEPHEN GOESER I
>
> On August 21, 1841, a year before Stephen Goeser and his family reached New York, Christian Güser (44) and his wife Gertrude (44) arrived there on the same ship, the Silvie de Grasse. With them, according to its passenger list, were their eight children -- Agnes (22), Joseph (20), Lorenzo (15), Peter (10), Anna (12), Theodore (8), Maria (3), and Anna (1). They were emigrants from Dümpelfeld in the Rhineland, as we know from the record in St. John's Church, Johnsburg, Wi., of the marriage Nov. 25, 1848, of Anna Marie Güser, daughter of "defuncti Chrysanti Güser et viventi Gertrudis Prinz, ex parochia Dümpelfeld, circuli Adenavenis" (See Appendix, p. 3). The church records of Dümpelfeld, available on microfilm from the Mormon Genealogical Library, give us much information about the family prior to its departure for America. Chrysanth, according to the record of his marriage (See Appendix, p. 16), was the son of Anthony Goeser and Catherine Fingsheim of Bouderath, and in all probability the brother of Stephen. His wife was the daughter of John Prinz and Gertrude Weber of Hahnensteinmühl in the parish of Dümpelfeld. Eleven children were born to them in Dümpelfeld. Typical of the baptismal records is the first one: "1815-31 Martii in facie Ecclesiae, baptizata fuit Chrysanthi Güser, et Annae Gertrudis Prinz conjugum, ex mola farinaria Hanenstein legitima filia Anna Gertrud," which translated reads, "Baptized in the sight of the church, on March 13, 1851, was Anna Gertrud, legitimate daughter of Chrysanth

This old manuscript was captured using the Evernote built-in camera. It's now indexed and easily searchable.

POWER-USER TIP

Playing the Waiting Game

When you photograph documents, you unleash the power of Evernote's indexing on them. They'll be searchable based on the text in the photo. But this process can take a few minutes, or even longer if you're adding a lot of documents at once. That's because the actual indexing takes place on Evernote's servers, and server load times can vary. If you've just uploaded a bunch of documents and are wondering why the search feature isn't working, that's the culprit. Grab a beverage, read a genealogy article or two, and it will be done before you know it.

2. Open your Finder (on a Mac) or File Explorer (on a PC), then open Evernote. As with photos, this is easiest if you open both windows at the same time, so you may need to resize your windows to fit them on your screen simultaneously.

3. Drag the scanned document files into an open Evernote note. You can choose to add one photo per note or include several that relate to each other in a single note.

4. Type in whatever notes and/or tags make sense for each document. Again, if you're working with documents, you may not have to add much, since printed text will be indexed and searchable.

Annotating Documents and Photos

Once your documents are in Evernote, you might wish to annotate them—mark them up with notes, circles, arrows and other elements. Annotation is great for calling attention to certain parts of a document, reminding yourself why a particular element was important, or adding supplemental notes such as follow-up questions or research theories. Evernote allows you to easily annotate photo and documents. Let's walk through the options.

THE ANNOTATION MENU

To get started, open up the note containing the image you want to annotate, then right-click on the picture (image **K**). You'll end up in a new window. Your image will be on the right, and an icon menu will appear on the left. Here's what each icon does (see labels on image **L**):

1. The **arrow tool**, as you might expect, allows you to draw an arrow pointing to important people or data. Click and drag to make the arrow appear on the image. You can drag it around using your mouse if you need to relocate it.

2. The **text tool** (the lowercase a icon) allows you to insert a text box. You can use this for a variety of useful text (such as placing source citations onto a document).

3. The **rectangle tool** allows you to easily draw a thick box around a section of your photo. Click and drag to make it appear.

4. The **highlight tool** is like having a marker in your hand. Use it to draw freehand circles or text, just like you would with a real marker.

5. The **stamp tool** (it's the circle icon with an X inside and an arrow jutting out) creates a "stamp" with a built-in text box. You can change the X to a heart, exclamation point, question mark, or checkmark. It's akin to putting a little sticky note on the image.

6. The **blurring tool** is the icon that looks like a pixelated blob. If you're working with a document that has information about living people or other sensitive data, you can

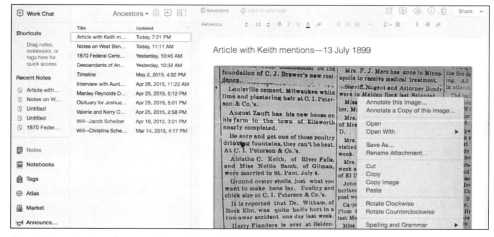

Annotating a photo or document image is easy in Evernote.

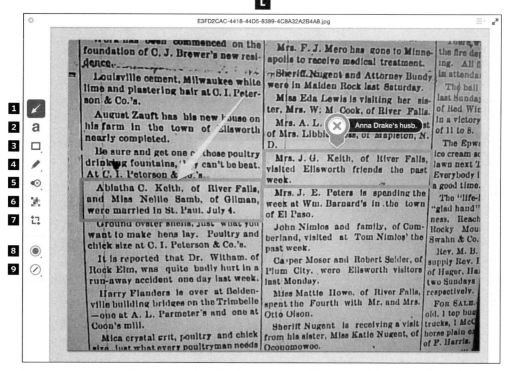

The annotation screen gives you a number of options. You can add arrows, text, boxes, and different types of arrows, blur out sensitive data, and crop the image as needed.

use it to blur that section out. This is great if you're going to be presenting the image to a wider audience at some point (in a blog post or on social media, for example).

7. The **cropping tool** is the box with the two plus signs on opposite corners. Use it to crop out the unneeded parts of your document or photo image. For instance, a record image from a genealogy website might have extra black space from when the record was scanned.

8. The **color selector** is the first dot icon. Use this to choose the color of your arrows, text boxes, and highlighter. You have a rainbow of colors to choose from to make your annotations stand out.

9. The **thickness selector** is the final box on the toolbar. Click it and you'll see a variety of thicknesses to choose from. Use this to choose the thickness of your arrows and the lines around your boxes.

MORE ANNOTATION OPTIONS

The icon at the top right corner with the three small horizontal lines is important as well. Click it and you'll see a pop-up menu with additional options. From this menu, you can perform the following actions (labeled on image **M**):

1. Clear all of your annotations and start over.

2. Reverse the image (that is, create a mirror image of your document).

3. Rotate the image (helpful if you've accidentally scanned or photographed the item sideways).

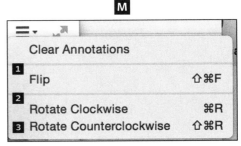

On the annotation screen, click the icon with the three small horizontal lines to see these additional options.

When you're done with your annotations, just click the X in the top left corner of the window. You'll return to your original note, which will now include all of the marks and notes you've added.

ADDING AUDIO FILES

It's one of the first pieces of advice a genealogist receives: Interview your older relatives. If you're fortunate enough to have relatives available to tell family stories, don't wait another day before talking to them about what they remember.

Of course, this is easier said than done. Not all of our relatives relish talking about the old days. Some feel like it's more of an intrusion than an opportunity to reminisce, and others may only be able to remember things on their good days.

Fortunately, Evernote can store your audio files should you be lucky enough to have them. By preserving the actual audio from interviews, Evernote helps you keep your ancestors around long after they're gone, and preserve their memories and life experiences in their own words. In this section, we'll look at some of the ways Evernote can preserve your ancestors' voices.

Recording Audio Files on Your Computer

If you have the luxury of setting up a time and date to interview a relative, conducting the interview using your computer or laptop is a great strategy. Because you're likely to have more storage space on your computer than on a mobile device, you'll have more room for a large audio file. You'll also have better options in terms of using a USB microphone, which can dramatically improve the sound quality of your interview. Here's how to create an audio file in Evernote on your desktop or laptop computer:

1. Plug in your microphone, if you're using one.

2. From the main menu, choose File, then New Audio Note.

3. Type in the title of your note, then enter any text you like. It's a good idea to include the names of the people you interviewed, the date and place the interview was conducted, and the material covered. This means you'll be able to easily find it again when you search for it, and you won't have to listen to the recording to determine what it's about long after you've forgotten what was covered.

4. Click the small microphone icon. It's in the toolbar just above the note text, the third item from the right.

5. The Record dialog toolbar will appear (image **N**). Click the blue Record button when you're ready to begin.

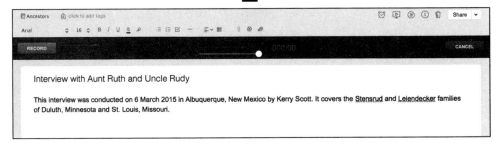

This is what your note will look like when you're ready to record.

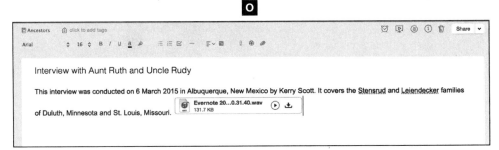

This is what your note will look like when you're finished recording.

6. You're on the air! Begin by identifying yourself, then identifying the other people in the room. You might know who they are, but whoever inherits this audio file may not.

7. When you've finished recording, click the red Save button. A box will appear in your note that indicates an audio file is part of the note (image O). Click the Play button to hear it.

8. The download link allows you to download the file and save it to your hard drive separately. It's a good idea to do that so you have a backup copy separate from your Evernote file. Interviews are nearly impossible to duplicate, so it's especially wise to keep multiple copies when you manage to conduct one. If you use an online backup service, be sure to save the recording in a folder that's scheduled to be backed up.

Recording Audio Files on Mobile Devices

Creating audio files on your computer is great, but it's a premeditated act. Few of us have the luxury of working with living relatives who perform on cue. More often, our opportunities to record storytelling relatives are more like lightning strikes—exciting, but hard to predict. Smartphones and tablets make it much more likely that we'll be ready for those bolts of serendipity, and Evernote allows us to record on the go. Here's how to capture the moment when a relative starts talking:

1. Open your Evernote app. Click the text icon to open a new text note (image 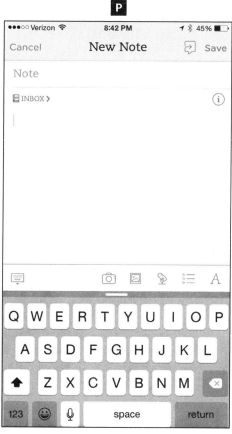).

2. Type in your important information about the interview—participants, location, and topics. If things are moving fast and you need to skip this to get to the recording because you might miss important information, don't worry. You can add it later. This is guerrilla genealogy: You have to be quick to get the good stuff.

3. Click the microphone icon. Your device will start recording instantly, so be ready.

Scouting an Interview Location

Capturing interviews on the fly is a tricky business. When you get someone in a sharing mood, you have to act fast. When you're recording from a mobile device, however, sound quality can be an issue. This is especially true if you're at a loud family function, such as a reunion or a party. I've found that you get the best sound quality if you can get people to sit in a room that has soft, upholstered furniture, carpeting, and/or drapes. For this reason, the living room or family room is often better than the kitchen or dining room. An empty bedroom is even better (although, admittedly, it's a little weird—but then, they already think you're weird, because you're a genealogist). Be strategic in where you ask your guests to sit if you're trying to get them to talk. They might look at you strangely, but you'll be glad you went to the trouble when you end up with an audio file that you can actually hear. There's nothing more frustrating than getting home and realizing you can't quite understand what Aunt Ruth was saying.

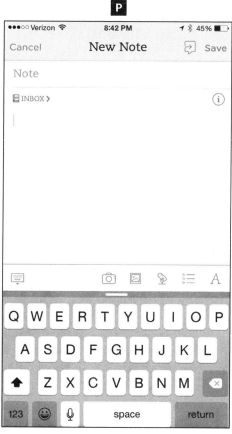

Open a new text note, then tap the microphone to start recording.

Mic Check

If you use a microphone to record your audio file on your computer or laptop, don't just plug it in and assume your computer will use it. Go into your computer's settings and check that your microphone is set to be the default input device. Without a microphone, your webcam is usually the device your computer will use to record sound, and the sound quality will be poor. You'll be disappointed if you talk into your microphone for an entire interview, only to find the sound didn't record through it because it wasn't set up properly. Check your settings first, then record a sample sentence or two to ensure it's working.

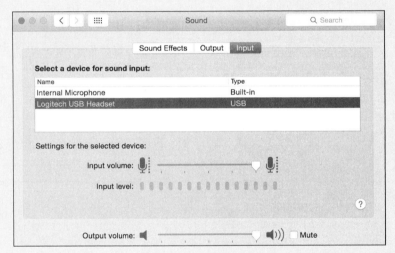

Be sure to double-check your default audio input device before you start interviewing.

4. Do your best to point the microphone on your device at the person speaking.

5. When the interview is over, click Done. Your note will include a box similar to the one in the desktop version of Evernote, and you'll see the audio file there. Click it to play the recording.

WORKING WITH PDF

What genealogy buff doesn't regularly work with PDFs? Many of our favorite genealogical magazines, journals, and newsletters arrive in PDF form. In fact, more and more genealogical societies are moving to electronic-only delivery for publications, so the number of PDFs genealogists receive is increasing.

If you order a pension file, obituary, or other document from a library or repository, you're likely to receive it via PDF. Even family tree programs allow you to save your descendant reports and ancestor charts in PDF form. What this means: Many of us have dozens (even hundreds) of PDFs lurking on our computers. There might even be quite a few that we've forgotten we have. Our senders don't always give the files names that make them easy to find later on, so they're hard to pull up in a search. They're in the digital equivalent of an unmarked grave. In short, they're useless, because they're hidden—and often forgotten.

Evernote changes this entire landscape. When you store PDFs in your notes, you can tag them so you can find them again. In fact, if you're a Premium subscriber, you'll be able to search the PDFs themselves. That means if you have a *National Genealogical Society Quarterly* from 1999, and it has an article on using records in Cattaraugus County, New York, you'll find it in 2016 when you suddenly discover ancestors in that county. You probably won't remember that article, but Evernote remembers for you. The more PDFs you store in Evernote, the more valuable your files become, because Evernote creates an instant index of all of your resources. It's an incredible tool for genealogists.

Here's how to add your PDFs to Evernote:

1. Download the PDFs from your e-mail, the website you're using, or the flash drive/CD you've stored them on. Make a note of where they end up. Most operating systems default to a folder called Downloads for items downloaded from e-mail or websites.

2. Open your Finder (on a Mac) or File Explorer (on a PC), then open Evernote. As with photos, this process is easiest if you have both windows open at the same time. You may need to make your windows smaller to fit them on your screen simultaneously.

3. Drag the PDF files into an open Evernote note. The note can be blank or already have content in it. You can do one PDF per note or include several that belong together (like all *National Genealogical Society Quarterly* issues, all digital *Family Tree Magazine* issues, etc.). Remember your maximum note size (25MB for Basic users, 50MB for Plus users, and 200MB for Premium users). Like photos and audio files, PDFs can be large, so check their size before adding too many to a single note.

4. Type in whatever accompanying notes you'd like and add tags as needed. If you're a Basic or Plus subscriber, it's important to tag the notes so you can find them again. If you're a Premium subscriber, the entire PDF will be indexed so you'll be able to find it later, even if you don't tag it.

Of course, if your PDF comes to you via e-mail, and you're a Plus or Premium subscriber, you can simply forward the e-mail to your special Evernote e-mail address. That will put the

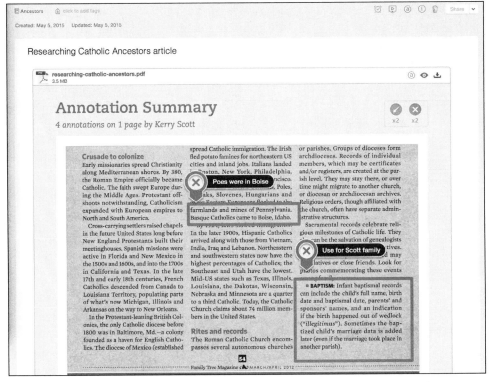

This article is annotated to highlight the parts that specifically relate to various lines of research.

e-mail and the PDF directly into an Evernote note. Use the @ sign in the subject line to designate the notebook (@NGSQ, for instance) and the # sign to add tags (as in #Cattaraugus). You can even set a reminder to read it by adding *!Reminder* to the subject line.

If you're a Premium subscriber, you can annotate your PDF (image). Annotation is a great way to highlight key points and remember which parts of a PDF relate to your research.

WEB CLIPPINGS

When I started doing genealogical research, the Internet was basically AOL and CompuServe. There were user groups devoted to genealogy, but there wasn't much in the way of actual records online.

Times have changed. Even most old-school genealogists now do at least a portion of their research online. The number of web-accessible records, images, and clues has exploded, and that means we need a way to capture them. For many years, that meant printing out stuff. Now we have the option of capturing images digitally—but that doesn't mean we will be able to find the source again.

Evernote has a tool called Web Clipper that allows users to capture images directly in a note. This is a huge breakthrough, because it means we can edit, annotate, and cross-reference those images. Have you ever downloaded an image of a census record and wondered which ancestor to file it under? If the people listed have different names (or changed their names, or might not even be your ancestors), what file name do you choose so you'll find them in this census record no matter what? You don't need to think about that anymore, because you can put the images in Evernote and tag them with as many names as you need to make them findable.

Installing the Web Clipper

The Web Clipper is a browser extension. That means it's a separate tool from Evernote itself, although it's designed by the same company. You'll need to install it in order to use it. The process of installation varies depending on your browser.

INSTALLING THE WEB CLIPPER IN FIREFOX

1. Navigate to <www.evernote.com/webclipper>.

2. Evernote will automatically determine that you're using Firefox. You'll see a green button that says Download to Firefox. Click it and the file will download.

3. When the download is complete, you'll see a message that says, "Evernote Web Clipper will be installed after you restart Firefox." Click the Restart Now button.

4. When Firefox reloads, you'll see the Evernote elephant in the toolbar.

INSTALLING THE WEB CLIPPER IN CHROME

1. Navigate to <www.evernote.com/webclipper>.

2. Evernote will automatically determine that you're using Chrome. You'll see a green button that says Download to Chrome. Click it, and the file will download automatically.

3. When the download is complete, you'll see a button that says Add. Click it, and you'll get a warning message telling you that Evernote will be able to access your browsing data. That's because it needs that access to capture the stuff in your browser window, as well as the URL (which you'll need for your source citation).

4. Once you've agreed to the installation, the Evernote elephant will appear in your Chrome toolbar.

INSTALLING THE WEB CLIPPER IN SAFARI

1. Navigate to **<www.evernote.com/webclipper>**.

2. Evernote will automatically determine that you're using Safari. You'll see a green button that says Download for Safari. Click it, and the file will download automatically.

3. Go to your Downloads file and double-click the new Evernote Web Clipper file. It will unzip, then ask you whether you'd like to install it. Click Install.

4. You'll see the Evernote elephant in the Safari toolbar when installation is complete.

INSTALLING THE WEB CLIPPER IN INTERNET EXPLORER

Internet Explorer has a special relationship with Evernote. When you download the desktop version of Evernote (which we did in chapter 2), the Web Clipper is automatically added to Internet Explorer as part of the installation process. You probably won't see it, though, unless you go into Internet Explorer's settings and enable the Command Bar (the bar that shows you various tools for your browser, including Web Clipper). Here's how to enable the Command Bar:

1. Open Internet Explorer.

2. Place your mouse pointer somewhere in the middle of the browser screen, then right-click. A pop-up menu will appear.

3. The third menu option will be Command Bar. Click it. You'll now see the Evernote elephant in your Internet Explorer toolbar.

Using the Web Clipper

Now that you have the Web Clipper installed, the fun part starts. This is where you actually find something valuable on the Internet and clip it right into Evernote. There are a number of Evernote moments where you feel like you're living in an episode of *The Jetsons*, but web clipping is particularly prone to make you appreciate twenty-first-century technology. Here's how to use the Web Clipper:

1. Navigate to the page that has data you want to clip.

It's All Related

Because I'm a Premium Evernote subscriber, I have access to the Related Content feature in Evernote. With this feature, Evernote identifies notes that the program believes to be related to other notes you've saved. For example, when I created the screenshot of the Thomas Goodier page for this book, I got a message after I clicked Save. It showed me records from my own files that Evernote believed might be related to Thomas Goodier. In this case, Evernote was right—these notes all relate to this ancestor. This feature becomes more intuitive the more you use it (and the more notes you create), and it's a highly underrated benefit of Premium membership. Think of it as the equivalent of the Ancestry.com shaky leaf for Evernote.

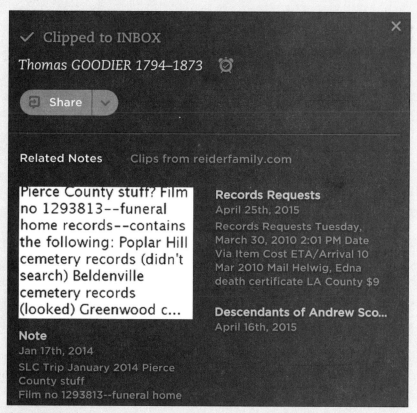

Evernote's Related Content can help you cross-reference your saved material.

Quick Guide to Clipping Options

The Web Clipper lets you capture a variety of web content. You can choose from these options:

- **Article:** This will capture the entire page. This includes the information at the bottom of the page (so you don't have to scroll down) but excludes the website's header and footer.

- **Simplified Article:** This will pull the whole article you're looking at, excluding the header, footer, and sidebars (including ads and those blinky graphics you still see on some blogs and older websites).

- **Full Page:** This captures everything. When in doubt, use this option so you don't miss important points—especially if you're working with a blog post that has important comments you want to save.

- **Bookmark:** As the name implies, this creates a bookmark that will land in your Evernote note. There will be a little snippet of text so you have some sense as to what the bookmark relates to. Keep in mind, though, that all of your clippings will have a link back to the original site, so don't pick the Bookmark selection unless you want only the bookmark and snippet.

- **Screenshot:** This copies the entire web page. Screenshot is a good option if you want to crop different parts using Evernote's annotation features. For example, if you're looking at a county map that shows townships, you might choose the Screenshot option, then crop out the specific townships you want to capture.

Once you've made your selections, click the big green Save button. Your clipping is now in Evernote and ready to use. At the top of the clipping, you'll see the date it was clipped, along with a link to the original website. Clicking that link takes you to the exact page this clipping came from (not just the home page), which makes creating source citations from web-based sources a breeze.

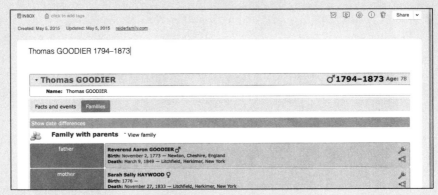

This screen clipping has been saved to Evernote.

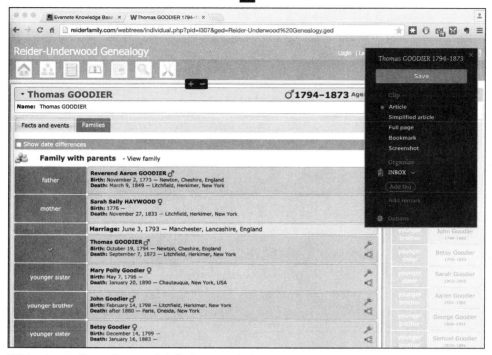

This is what you'll see when you click the Evernote elephant icon.

2. Click the Evernote elephant icon in your browser's toolbar. A pop-up menu will appear with lots of options (image **R**).

3. Under Clip, you'll have some choices to make regarding the scope of the clipping you want. See the sidebar Quick Guide to Clipping Options for a rundown.

4. Under Organize, you'll have more options. If you've set your INBOX notebook to be your default, you'll see that this clipping is slated to end up there. You can change that, though, by clicking INBOX and choosing a different notebook. Click Add Tag or Add Remark to put in notes and tags that relate to this clipping.

5. Under Options, you can make some global changes to how web clippings are handled (image **S**). Note that these settings apply to all of your web clippings, not just the one you're currently working on.

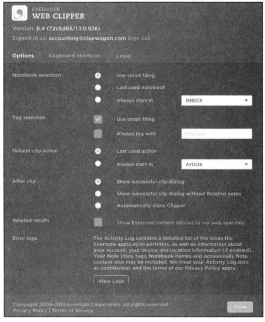

Reaching Into the Internet's Past

Sometimes you find great information on a website—then the website disappears. Evernote captures the URL for each web clipping you create, but that may seem like cold comfort if the original website is no longer online. The Internet Archive's Wayback Machine **<www.archive.org>** (named after Mr. Peabody's time machine from the TV show *Rocky and Bullwinkle*) is an invaluable resource when this happens. This website stores old copies of websites, including sites that have been offline for years. Since you have the URL from Evernote, you can check the Wayback Machine to pull up the archived copy of the original website.

The Options link allows you to make global changes to how you want to manage web clippings.

KEYS to SUCCESS

* Add all kinds of genealogical content to your Evernote file. Evernote can handle text notes, handwritten notes, audio files, e-mails, PDFs, and clippings from websites. If you have material of genealogical value, there's likely a way to get it into a note.

* Use Evernote as a central repository for all your genealogy research, because the software is most valuable when you use it for *everything*. If you have all of your data in one place, you can find it and cross-reference it. You can use tags (see chapter 5) to analyze data, and if you're a Premium subscriber, you can use the Related Content feature to look for clues you've forgotten all about.

* Subscribe to Evernote Premium to take advantage of some of the best features for organizing genealogy materials. The ability to search and annotate PDFs is particularly valuable, and the Related Content feature can help you spot clues you may have missed.

Sharing and Collaborating

We genealogists love our dead people. Sooner or later, though, we have to work with living relatives in order to further our research. The recent addition of DNA to genealogists' toolboxes has made this even clearer. After all, every one of our DNA matches is a living person who we'll need to work with to find our connection. Each branch of the family may have different stories, photos, documents, and bits of information. Keeping track of all of those clues can be a daunting task.

Fortunately, Evernote allows us to create a flexible, collaborative working space that's easy to use, even for our less tech-savvy cousins. You can share notebooks or individual notes, depending on what makes sense for the project you're working on. Many genealogists have shared family trees on various platforms for years, but being able to share your actual work space opens up a whole new range of possibilities. In this chapter, we'll explore those possibilities and show you how to take your genealogical collaboration to a whole new level with Evernote.

Going the Distance

The ability to share notes can be especially powerful when combined with Evernote's sync capabilities. Not long ago, I had a cousin who lived across the country from me. He visited the National Archives and Records Administration **<www.archives.gov>** in Washington, DC, to review a pension file for one of our shared ancestors. He typed notes into a notebook we were sharing and took photos of each page of the pension file as he reviewed it. Because his Evernote file was syncing, and I was also syncing with the shared notebook at home, I was able to follow his progress in real time.

I was able to pay it forward a few weeks later, when I visited a cemetery in New Mexico for someone who lives in New England. She was able to see the headstones I photographed while I was still standing there, because I took the photos in our shared Evernote note. Sharing can quite literally bridge the distance between you and your collaborating cousins.

COLLABORATION OPPORTUNITIES IN EVERNOTE

The ways you can work with others via Evernote are pretty much limited only by your imagination. Anything you want to collaborate on is fair game. For example, you and your research partner (or partners) can use Evernote for

- notes on how you think a particular family might be related;
- a shared research log that allows you to divvy up the work without duplicating any of it;
- photos of documents gathered in the course of your research efforts, with annotations to allow you to point out key information;
- lists of microfilm rolls you need to order to find out more about your shared ancestors so you can divide and conquer;
- maps pinpointing the exact location of a grave or home, or showing migration routes or homes of related individuals;
- web clippings from clues you've found on the Internet;
- copies of audio files of interviews done with older relatives from long-lost branches of the family;
- photos of individuals (a great way to put your heads together and figure out who those people you don't recognize might be);
- photos of heirlooms that other branches of the family may not have seen for generations;
- plans for genealogical society conferences, events, and projects;
- notes on DNA cousins who match both of you; and

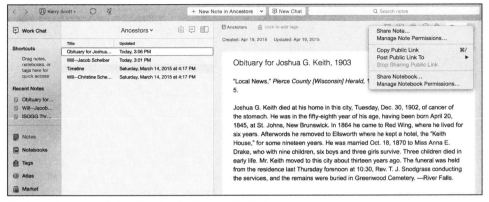

Start your Evernote collaborations by sharing an individual note.

- information you're sharing with a professional genealogist, librarian, or volunteer you're working with.

One thing you'll need to consider is which platform is best suited for sharing with the particular person you're working with. We all know a person who seems to be on Facebook **<www.facebook.com>**, Instagram **<www.instagram.com>**, and Twitter **<www.twitter.com>** all day long and someone else who flatly refuses to use any social media. Evernote sharing is available via a variety of platforms, so you can tailor your sharing method to the needs (or quirks) of the person you're working with. That's a big help when you're trying to get a reluctant cousin to collaborate. You can share notes or notebooks via the following methods:

- Facebook
- Twitter
- LinkedIn **<www.linkedin.com>**
- text messaging (SMS)
- e-mail
- public link (that is, a link you can copy and paste into whatever format you want, including a blog, a newsletter, an Ancestry.com private message, or any other tool that meets your needs)

Now that I've given you ideas for the type of teamwork that's possible with Evernote, let's look at how to start sharing and collaborating.

SHARING INDIVIDUAL NOTES

Most users start working with others in Evernote by sharing an individual note (image **A**). It's a logical entry point, and you can do it via e-mail, link, social media, and text message.

Sharing a Note via E-mail

E-mail is a medium most genealogists use frequently for their research work, so sharing a note this way is a no-brainer for many potential collaborators. And for those who aren't active social media users or text messagers, e-mail is an ideal way to share. The process involves seven steps.

1. Navigate to the individual note you want to share.

2. Click on the down arrow on the Share button. You'll see several options.

3. Click Share Note, then enter the e-mail address of the person you want to share with.

4. At the top of the dialog box (image **B**), enter the e-mail address of the person you're sending the note to.

5. At the bottom of the dialog box, you'll see the words "Take a look at this note." That's the default text that will be inserted into the e-mail you're sending. You can alter this message and or delete it and type in one of your own.

6. Just above the default language, you'll see the name of the note you're sending. Next to that, there's a menu to choose the level of permission you want to grant to the person you're sending the note to. Click that to make changes. If you choose Can View, your recipient will be able to look at the note but won't be able to make changes. Select Can

POWER-USER TIP

Adding Gmail Contacts

If you're a Gmail user, you're in luck, because Evernote has a special relationship with Gmail. You can choose to link your Google Contacts to your Evernote account. This speeds things up considerably when e-mailing your cousins and other research colleagues, and ensures that you won't accidentally type in the wrong e-mail address. To enable this feature, start from the e-mail dialog box. Begin typing in an e-mail address. You'll see a pop-up box right below it that says, Link Google Contacts. Click on that, then follow the prompts to link your preferred Gmail account. When you're finished, you'll have access to all of your saved e-mail contacts right in Evernote.

The dialog box for sharing a note via e-mail lets you specify what your recipient can do with your note.

Edit if you want the recipient to be able to view the note and make changes. Or if you'd like to give your recipient total access—allowing her to do everything you can, including read the note, edit it, and invite her own friends—pick Can Edit and Invite.

7. When you've made all of your selections, click Send.

Sharing a Note via a Link

Sometimes you'll want to share a link to your note in a blog post, newsletter, Ancestry.com source note, or another document. To do this, follow these four steps:

1. Navigate to the individual note you want to share.

2. Click on the down arrow on the Share button.

3. Click Copy Public Link. The link will be added automatically to your clipboard.

4. Paste the link into the appropriate document. Anyone with the link will be able to access your note.

Sharing a Note via LinkedIn

It might seem strange to think about sharing a genealogy note on LinkedIn, the popular social networking website for professionals. This sharing option is obviously designed for the many business users of Evernote. But if you belong to genealogy networking groups on LinkedIn, you might find that it makes complete sense to share an exciting find or ask for a second opinion on how to interpret something. LinkedIn also can be helpful for finding long-lost cousins who aren't on other social media sites, and you may well wish to share notes with those cousins at some point. In fact, if your cousin is a business leader or other prominent person, LinkedIn might be the only social media site where she has a profile. Here's how to share a note via LinkedIn:

1. Navigate to the individual note you want to share.

2. Click on the down arrow on the Share button.

3. Hover your mouse over Post Public Link To, then choose LinkedIn.

4. If you're not already logged in to LinkedIn, you'll be prompted to do that. After a pause, a new window will open, and you'll see the LinkedIn sharing dialog box.

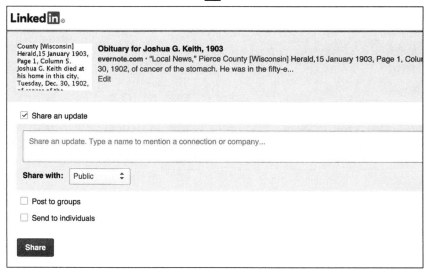

This is what you'll see when you share a note on LinkedIn.

5. Type in any special message you'd like to share along with the note. Under Share with, you can choose Public (meaning everyone can see the note and message) or Connections (meaning only the people you're directly connected to on LinkedIn can see them). You also can choose to post to one or more groups (say, your favorite genealogy networking group) or to send it only to individuals (such as that long-lost cousin you just found).

6. When you've made your selections, click the Share button to send the note (image C).

Choose Share on Facebook in the top left corner of your note.

If you share your note on your Facebook Timeline, you can choose who sees it and who doesn't.

Sharing a Note via Facebook

Facebook is a hugely popular tool among genealogists. It's a great place to connect with cousins, find others researching in the locations where your ancestors lived, and get help with your brick-wall research problems. For that reason, it's entirely likely that you'll want to share an Evernote note with some or all of your Facebook friends at some point. Here's how to do it:

1. Navigate to the individual note you want to share.

2. Click on the down arrow on the Share button.

3. Hover your mouse over Post Public Link To, then choose Facebook.

4. Once you're logged in to Facebook, you'll see the sharing dialog box (image **D**). At the top, you'll be able to choose where to share the note: On your own Timeline (the place where you'd normally share a post or photo with your friends), On a friend's Timeline, In a group, On a Page you manage, or In a private message.

Your Evernote note will appear on your Facebook Timeline, just like it does when you share any other web link. Your friends can click through to see the note.

5. When you've chosen the method of sharing, the dialog box will disappear and you'll be able to type in your own message to go along with the link to your note.

6. If you choose to share on your own timeline, you'll want to review the list of people who can see it. To do this, click on the button right next to Cancel to see a drop-down menu of choices (image **E**): Public allows anyone with Internet access to see your note. Friends gives access only to people you're Facebook friends with. Only Me means no one but you can see it. Custom lets you pick and choose who can see the note by listing people you want to include/exclude.

7. Once you've made your selection, click Share Link to post to Facebook. Image **F** shows how this displays when you share the link on your timeline.

Sharing a Note via Twitter

Twitter is an especially good tool for crowdsourcing—that is, getting lots of people to weigh in on your research question or problem. If you're looking to get help on interpreting old handwriting or determining if two people in old photos might be one and the same, Twitter's global reach makes it a great resource. Here's how to share a note on Twitter:

1. Navigate to the individual note you want to share.

The dialog box for sharing your note via Twitter is quite simple.

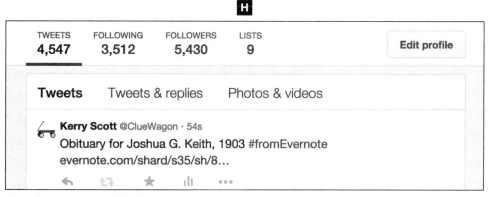

This is how your tweet will look if you stick with the default settings.

2. Click on the down arrow on the Share button.

3. Hover your mouse over Post Public Link To, then choose Twitter. A dialog box will appear (image G).

4. Review the default text. You'll notice that your tweet automatically will be hashtagged #fromEvernote. If that's not a fit for you, you can delete the hashtag or replace it with something more useful (such as #genealogy or #history). And don't worry about the length of the link; Twitter will truncate it for you automatically.

5. When you've adjusted your tweet to your liking, click Tweet to send it (image H).

Sharing a Note via Text Message

There are times when fast just isn't fast enough. When you're at a research repository, a cemetery, or another important location, you might need to share something with a cousin instantly. In those cases, sharing via text messaging is probably your fastest option. Since

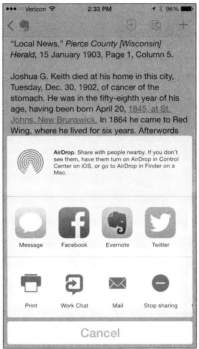

On an iPhone, select Messaging from the note-sharing dialog box to share a note via text message.

POWER-USER TIP

An Apple Advantage

If you're on iOS 8.0 or later, you'll be able to send your note via iMessage rather than SMS texting. This means you can send it to devices that don't necessarily have cellular connections, as long as the person on the other end has an Apple ID set up. It also means your iMessage settings (such as read receipts) will apply.

this sort of situation comes up primarily when you're on the go, Evernote allows sharing via text message only from mobile devices, not from the desktop or web versions. Here's how to share from your mobile device:

1. Open Evernote on your mobile device.

2. Navigate to the individual note you want to share.

3. Tap the three little dots in the lower right corner of your screen, then tap Share.

4. You'll see the share dialog box open up (image **I** shows this on an iPhone). The specific options will vary based on your platform and individual device settings, but you'll see a Message or Text option. Tap it.

5. Evernote will prompt you to choose whether you want to share a public link (accessible by anyone) or a private link (accessible only to the person you're sending it to). Tap the one you want to choose.

6. Enter the phone number of the person you want to text your link to, then tap Send.

Popular Genealogy Facebook Groups

If you don't already belong to any genealogy-focused groups on Facebook, you'll find they're wonderful forums for sharing ideas and tips (and convenient if you're going to be on Facebook anyway). Some popular groups that may be of interest to you:

- Evernote Genealogists
- The Organized Genealogist
- Technology for Genealogy
- Find A Grave
- DNA Detectives
- Genealogy! Just ask!

To find these groups, search for the name on Facebook. Also search for groups for your ancestors' state and ethnic heritage. Once you're in a few genealogy groups and connected to other genealogists, Facebook will recommend other related groups (click Groups, then Suggested Groups to view them). Don't see a group for your pet topic? Consider creating your own.

SHARING ENTIRE NOTEBOOKS

For some projects, sharing an individual note just isn't enough. You may be working on a larger project or with a big group and have multiple bits of information to share. In those cases, it might make more sense to use a shared notebook.

Sharing whole notebooks works much like sharing notes, but with more limitations on what you can do. Here are the key differences between sharing a notebook and sharing individual notes:

- You can share a notebook from your desktop or laptop computer, but not from a mobile device. Notes can be shared from either place.

- Notebooks can be shared via e-mail, but there's no direct way to share via LinkedIn, Twitter, Facebook, or text messaging. As a practical matter, you can still share via those services by simply sending/posting a link to the notebook, but there won't be a handy dialog box to help you do it.

Here's how to share a notebook; the steps and options are labeled on image **J** for you to follow along:

1. Navigate to the list of notebooks on the left side of the screen.

2. Hover your mouse over the share icon on the notebook you want to share (it's next to the notebook title). Click it.

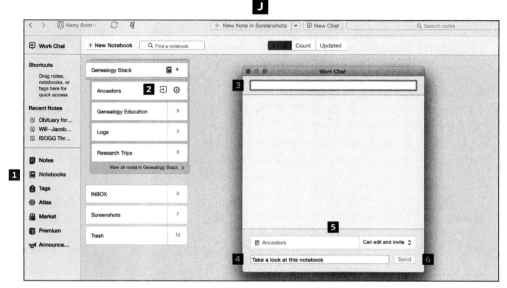

Sharing a notebook is similar to sharing an individual note.

3. At the top of the dialog box, enter the e-mail address of the person you're sending the note to.

4. At the bottom of the dialog box, you'll see "Take a look at this notebook." That's the default text that will be inserted into the e-mail you're sending. You can alter or delete this message, and type in one of your own.

5. Just above the default language, you'll see the name of the note you're sending. Next to that, there's a menu to choose the level of permission you want to grant to the person you're sending the note to. Click that to make changes: If you choose Can view, your recipient will be able to look at the note but won't be able to make changes. Select Can edit if you want the recipient to be able to view the note and make changes. Or to give your recipient total access—allowing her to do everything you can, including read the note, edit it, and invite her own friends—pick Can edit and invite.

6. When you've made all of your selections, click Send.

If you'd like to create a link to a notebook that you can share on social media or in a document, blog post, or newsletter, follow these steps:

1. Navigate to the list of notebooks on the left side of the screen.

2. Hover your mouse over the notebook you want to share, then right-click (control-click on Macs).

3. Choose Publish Notebook from the drop-down menu that appears (image **K**).

You can create a public link to a notebook to share wherever you like.

4. Click Publish. Evernote will generate a link to your notebook.

5. Copy and paste the link wherever you need to share it. If you change your mind or want to unpublish it later on, follow these same steps, then click Delete Public Link to revoke access.

VIEWING NOTE HISTORY

Collaborating with others on genealogical research is a delicate exercise. Sometimes our research leads us to information that our cousins would rather keep under wraps. Other times, we're working with people with varying degrees of skills (both in genealogical research and in using a computer). That can sometimes lead to erroneous conclusions or sloppy work. Occasionally, this can even lead to conflict. Sharing notes can be similar to sharing an online family tree in that others can make changes we don't necessarily agree with.

In this respect, Evernote is an especially great tool for the sometimes-dicey dance of genealogical collaboration. It offers the ability to view the note history so you can see

What About Stacks?

Unfortunately, as of this writing, Evernote doesn't allow users to share stacks. This is an often-requested feature, so it's entirely possible it will be added to future versions of Evernote. In the meantime, you can get around this limitation by sharing each notebook within a stack. It's a bit tedious, but it gets the job done.

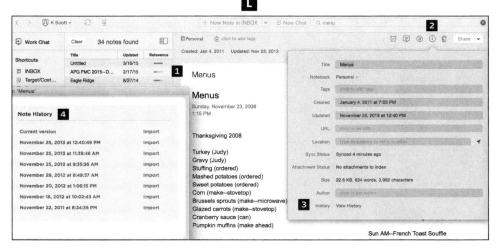

The note history is valuable for seeing exactly what changes were made to a document on a given date.

exactly what your cousins did to that note you shared. Here's how to view the note history (the steps are labeled on image **L** for your reference):

1. Open the note you want to review.

2. Click the note information icon (it's the circled lowercase letter-i in the top menu toolbox above the note).

3. You'll see a number of statistics about your note. At the bottom, there's a link to View History. Click it.

4. You'll see a list of previously saved versions of your note. Click Import to look at the one that corresponds to the date of the version you want to review.

USING PRESENTATION MODE

Every genealogist fights the same battle to get the rest of the relatives interested in family history. We all know that look: Your relatives' eyes glaze over, and they start looking for an escape route. Of course, we get why that probate file is so exciting or why that trip to the cemetery was a game changer, but it's often a tough sell with the wider world.

As any successful marketer will tell you, sometimes it's all in the packaging. That's why Evernote's Presentation Mode is so powerful for family historians. It allows you to make fancy presentations to share with your family without using expensive, complicated tools such as Microsoft PowerPoint. Imagine showing up at the next family reunion or Thanksgiving dinner with a slick presentation on your phone, laptop, or tablet. You'll easily attract even the most genealogically resistant relatives to the world of family history. Even the teenagers won't mind staring at your device for a bit.

Turning a note with multiple bits of information into a presentation takes just two steps:

1. Navigate to the note you want to work with.

2. Choose the presentation icon (a little screen with a right-arrow play button: see image **M**).

Voilà! Your screen will turn into a presentation screen. When you move your mouse, you'll see that it's been transformed into a pointer so it looks like a little comet streaking across your screen. That's handy for circling relevant information as you're talking about it. You can hit the space bar to scroll down at set intervals, or press shift+space to scroll

M

Starting Presentation Mode is as simple as clicking the button.

N

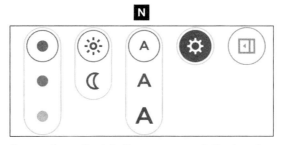

You can change the defaults on your presentation to make it a better fit for your audience and viewing situation.

back up (alternatively, you can just use the scroll wheel on your mouse, if you have one, or your arrow keys on a full-sized keyboard). To exit Presentation Mode, hit the Escape key.

You have a number of settings you can use to change the look of your presentation. To see them, move your mouse to the upper right corner, then click the gear icon. You'll see several options pop up (image **N**):

- On the left, you can change the color of the mouse pointer from the default (blue) to pink or green.

- In the center, you can switch to night view by clicking the moon icon. This will change the background from white to black, making it easier to see in darker conditions. If you're on a laptop or device that isn't plugged into a power source, this will also help a bit with battery life, since the laptop display doesn't have to use as much power for light.

- On the right, you can increase the font size from the default (small) to medium or large. The largest size is really quite large, making it a good fit for a big room or a relative who may not have great vision.

Of course, it's likely that you'll want to spruce up your note to make the most of your presentation. The default mode for Evernote presentations turns your note into one big, long screen to scroll through. You can choose to divide it into screens so each part is its own slide. That makes it easier for your viewers to digest the information, and it helps to guide your discussion points so you can ensure you're not leaving out key information. Here's how to easily add screen breaks:

1. Start Presentation Mode, move your mouse to the upper right corner, then click the Presentation Layout button (image **O**) that appears on the far right.

2. You'll see a large version of your presentation on the left and a filmstrip-like version on the right (image **P**). If you look closely, you'll see little blue dots on the far right. Those are the points at which you can add screen breaks to note where one slide should end and a new one should begin. Click the blue dot that's in the place you want to create a break. It will create a blue line. The line will be invisible during your actual presentation; it's just there to show you where the screen break will occur.

3. Once you've created your screen breaks, test out your presentation. If you don't like the way it looks, you can drag the blue lines to the places you want them. If you want to remove one altogether, click the minus sign on the far right next to the blue line.

Too much trouble? No problem. You can use the Auto Layout button (image **Q**) to do all of this for you. When you click it, Evernote will automatically divide your images into separate screens. It'll even create a title page for you.

O

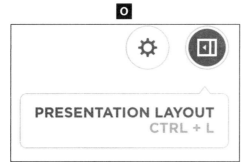

The Presentation Layout button takes you to a screen where you can create screen breaks for your presentation.

P

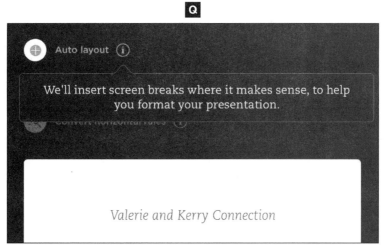

Click the tiny blue dots on the far right to create screen breaks. The dots will convert to thin blue lines that show where the screen breaks will occur.

Q

Use the Auto Layout feature to automatically create screen breaks based on the natural flow of the images in your note.

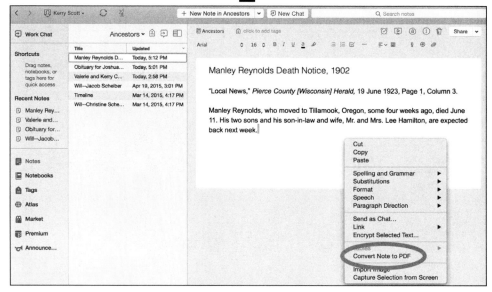

Evernote for Mac allows you to convert notes to PDF in one click.

CONVERTING NOTES TO PDF

Sharing Evernote files is a great idea—for most people. For a few, though, it's just not feasible. If you're working with a cousin who has trouble figuring out how to turn on the computer, walking him through a process even as easy as Evernote sharing might be too much. In those cases, it may make more sense to convert a note to PDF. This is a format that even beginning computer users can generally figure out how to open, so it's as close as you can get to a universal sharing format (aside from a old-fashioned paper printout, of course).

As of this writing, Evernote for Windows doesn't directly convert notes to PDF, so you'll need to do this via a PDF printer (though it's very likely that future versions will have this much-requested feature). The latest version of Evernote for Mac, though, allows you to convert a note to PDF right in the application. Here's how to do it:

1. Open the note you want to convert to PDF.

2. Navigate the mouse to somewhere on the note itself, then right-click. Choose Convert Note to PDF from the drop-down menu that appears (image).

3. In a second or two, your list of notes will include a duplicate of the one you're working on, with the same name. Open it and you'll see that it's a PDF.

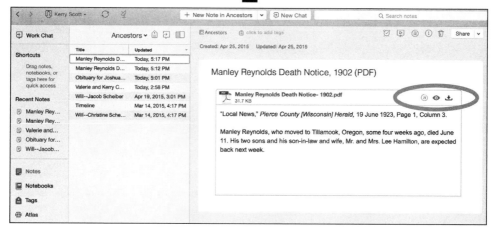

Once your note is converted to PDF, use the icons in the top-left corner to annotate, view, or save the PDF elsewhere on your computer.

4. In the top-right corner of the PDF box, you'll see three options (image **S**): The circled letter-a icon allows you to annotate the PDF. You can learn more about this in chapter 6. The eyeball icon allows you to view the PDF. The download icon allows you to save the PDF to your hard drive. You can then e-mail it to your cousin or add it to a flash drive or CD.

KEYS to SUCCESS

✳ Share individual notes or notebooks, depending on the size and scope of your project.

✳ Choose the method of sharing that best suits the person you're working with. Evernote works smoothly with e-mail, text messaging, Facebook, LinkedIn, and Twitter.

✳ Remember that you're not limited to the options Evernote gives you. You can generate a link to a note or notebook and share it anywhere you like.

✳ Use the Note History to see when changes were made and to restore older versions of the note if you need to.

✳ Presentation Mode is a great way to show others all of your great genealogy finds in a friendly, polished way. You have a variety of options to make your presentation look great and hold your audience's attention.

✳ Convert your notes to PDF if you want to share them in a format that even your least computer-savvy cousins can work with.

Putting It All Together

I gave a talk to a local genealogical society not long ago. It was an introduction to Evernote, with an overview of some of the cool things you could do with it. When the talk was over, a number of attendees approached me and said they'd had Evernote for some time, but they'd never actually used it. "I opened it up," one said, "but then I wasn't sure what I was supposed to *do*."

This is the thing about a new tool: It's not always clear how to fit it into your existing routine.

This chapter is meant to inspire you. In it, we'll talk about a variety of things genealogists might do in Evernote. You can use some of these ideas, just a few, or none at all. The goal is to get your creative juices flowing so you can begin to picture Evernote figuring into your own unique way of conducting your family history research. Ready? Let's go.

TABLES: A GREAT PLACE TO GET STARTED

Here's a confession: When I can't sleep, I shop. There are women who shop for shoes or purses online (or maybe via a home shopping channel). I'm not one of those at all. I shop

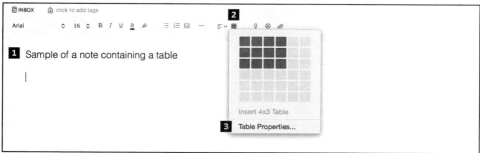

Click the grid icon to create a table to your specifications.

online for death certificates. Or marriage records. If I want instant gratification, I'll order a birth record. My native state (Minnesota) offers easy online shopping for all three of these, and its birth records can even be downloaded instantly. It's the home shopping channel for dead people, and I love it. There's only one problem: Once in a while, I'd order the same record twice. Death certificates aren't like shoes; you won't necessarily recognize one you ordered a year ago.

That's why the very first thing I created in Evernote was a correspondence log. I realized that if I didn't carefully track what I'd ordered, I'd end up bankrupt.

Shortly afterward, I realized I could use the same basic technique to create a research log. I'd had one on paper for years, but I found it clunky to use. If you were researching more than one line, who did you file the record or activity with? What about when people changed names? What about when I found a new line in the course of my research?

Then I learned to create census forms. Instead of hand-transcribing the census, I entered the data into my Evernote forms. Now I could search every word of every entry. This meant that I could look for all of the doctors, all of the farmers, all of the people with parents born in England—whatever I wanted. It was (and is) one of my favorite uses of Evernote.

Creating a Form

To do all of this, of course, you need to create forms. You could enter information freestyle (in paragraph form), but that would be messy. Most of us prefer the structure of a form for these kinds of applications.

Forms in Evernote are made out of tables, so you'll first need to know how to create a table. The process takes three steps, as shown on image :

1. Open your note and type in a title. Hit Enter to move down to the note entry area.

2. Choose the grid icon in the toolbar. Use your mouse to choose the size of the table you want.

3. Use the Table Properties link to create a larger table (more than six columns and/or six rows). You also can choose the thickness and color of the table border, change the alignment (left, center, or right), and alter the cell background color (which is white by default). Hit Enter to create your table.

After creating your table, you can use your mouse to drag the borders to change the column width to meet your needs. The row height will auto-adjust to accommodate the amount of text you enter in that row, so you don't need to spend time manually adjusting that dimension.

Creating a Correspondence Log

My correspondence log is one of my most-used Evernote forms. Every time I order a record, I add it to the log. If I write to a repository to ask about their collection, that goes into the log, too. If I e-mail a cousin or a DNA match, I enter that into the log. This way, I never have to try to remember if (or when) I talked to someone or whether I already tried getting the military file for a particular ancestor.

When I get a response, I enter that information, too. Over time, it's become a valuable resource for tracking how long I can expect to wait for a particular file. With five years of data, I now know that my average wait for a Minnesota death certificate is about nine days. In Wisconsin, it's about sixteen days for rural counties and thirty-three days for Milwaukee County. For an Oregon death certificate, I can expect to wait about twenty-six days. For a death record from Los Angeles County, I'm looking at about eight weeks. This helps me plan ahead and make the most efficient use of my time, whether I'm working on my own research or helping someone else. Sometimes I receive a response that tells me more about that repository's records, and I note that in my log. If the funeral home says their records are destroyed after seven years, I know not to request more records from it. I may not remember that tidbit five years from now, but Evernote never forgets.

I also track the cost of each record. This helps me see at a glance how much I've already spent from my genealogy budget, and how much I have left. It also serves as a handy reminder of how much records cost in a particular area so I can prioritize and plan accordingly.

To track all these details, I use the following headers in my correspondence log (see image **B**):

- **Date:** The specific day I made the request.

- **Via:** Was the item ordered via mail? Online? Through which website?

- **Item:** What was ordered, and who is the record for? Enter the full name of the person and the location, so you'll easily find it when you search your Evernote files.

Date	Via	Item	Cost	Notes
10 Mar 2010	Mail	Ackermann, Edna death certificate Los Angeles County	$9	Arrived 5 April 2010
30 Mar 2010	Mail	Helwig, Frederick E. SS-5	$35	Received 10 June 2010
2 Apr 2010	Mail	Ackermann, Mae death cert Huntington, Indiana	$8	Arrived 22 April 2010---not her
2 Apr 2010	Mail	Paulson, Edwin D death cert Portland, Oregon	$20	Arrived 13 Apr 2010
2 Apr 2010	Mail	Smith, Edward Lee death cert Los Angeles County	$12	Arrived 3 May 2010
2 Apr 2010	Mail	Hyatt, Mary Elizabeth death cert Los Angeles County	$12	Arrived 3 May 2010
2 Apr 2010	Mail	Hyatt, Leslie Jack death cert Los Angeles County	$12	Arrived 3 May 2010
6 Apr 2010	Mail	Ackermann, Edna marriage cert--Clark County, Nevada Recorder	$15	Arrived 16 April 2010
6 Apr 2010	Mail	Ackermann, Edna marriage lic and app--Clark County, Nevada	$8	Arrived 15 April 2010
6 Apr 2010	Mail	Jorgensen, Fred--Utter McKinley Mortuary (cemetery is not an option; prosecution for bad stuff)	$5	Arrived 22 April 2010--all records destroyed after 7 years
15 Apr 2010	Mail	Smith, Edward Lee coroner's report request for fee	$27	Arrived 23 April 2010
13 Apr 2010	NGS Website	Mhyre, Lawrence and Herbert--physician files from AMA	$30	Arrived 10 May 2010
28 Apr 2010	Mail	Thorbjorn, Charles Valden--death cert LA County	$12	Arrived 15 May 2010
28 Apr 2010	Mail	Schaeffer, Frank J/Ethel Morgan--marriage cert Hennepin County (tracking #053-00002107)	$9	Arrived 4 May 2010 (but only an abstract)
28 Apr 2010	Mail	Thorbjorn, Charles and Viola--Forest Lawn Cemetery records	None	Received via email 3 May 2010

I keep track of all my record requests in a correspondence log in Evernote.

- **Cost:** How much I spent on the record.
- **Notes:** This includes the date the item finally arrived, but also any quirks of the repository, information about further records' availability, etc. A few repositories (including the U.S. National Archives) provide a tracking number when you place an order online, so I put that in the notes as well.

A correspondence log is only as useful as the information you put in it. If you get in the habit of tracking every request, e-mail, and letter you send, you'll have a valuable, easily searchable resource for years to come.

Creating a Research Log

Research logs are supposed to be a staple of any effective genealogist's routine. We all know we should use them to track where we've looked and what we've found. We know that they will save us time and money by preventing us from looking in the same place twice. Research logs are the "eat your vegetables" of genealogy.

Of course, we don't always follow best practice. Instead, we go on Internet research binges and don't write down a thing, and a year later we end up looking in the same place again.

Evernote is like the cheese sauce that makes your vegetables taste better. It helps make the process easy and smooth so you can actually get into the habit of using a research log. Once you do, you'll realize that those experts were right: A research log really does save you time and money.

Date	Call Number	Description of Source	Purpose of Search	Results
11 March 2013		FamilySearch.org, Minnesota, County Birth Records 1863-1983 > Freeborn, Bath > Births, Deaths 1872-1896, Vol. A	Births or deaths of anyone with Hans/Barbara Peterson, Sigrid/Nils Nelson, Engebrit/Golete Erickson, Anna & Erick Arneson, Gjiskan and Lauritz Nelson, Nels/Kristine Nelson, Nels/Alice Nelson or Betsy/Christ Klavberg as parents; death of Karen Iverson	See files; death of Karen Iverson not found
26 March 2013		FamilySearch.org, Minnesota, County Birth Records 1863-1983 > Freeborn, Bath > Births, Deaths 1896-1900, Vol. B	Births or deaths of anyone with Hans/Barbara Peterson, Sigrid/Nils Nelson, Engebrit/Golete Erickson, Anna & Erick Arneson, Gjiskan and Lauritz Nelson, Nels/Kristine Nelson, Nels/Alice Nelson or Betsy/Christ Klavberg as parents; death of Karen Iverson or Hans and Barbara Peterson	See files (one birth to Lauritz and Gjisken Nelson). Hans not found in Bath township (probably in Albert Lea or "east of town" where he died). Barbara not found.
26 March 2013		FamilySearch.org, Minnesota, County Birth Records 1863-1983 > Freeborn, Bath > Births, Deaths 1900-1907, Vol. C	Births or deaths of anyone with Hans/Barbara Peterson, Sigrid/Nils Nelson, Engebrit/Golete Erickson, Anna & Erick Arneson, Gjiskan and Lauritz Nelson, Nels/Kristine Nelson, Nels/Alice Nelson or Betsy/Christ Klavberg as parents; death of Karen Iverson or Barbara Peterson	See files--one death, Luella Josephine Nelson). Barbara not found.
26 March 2013		FamilySearch.org, Minnesota, County Birth Records 1863-1983 > Freeborn > Birth Index, 1870-1920, Vol. A	All Nelson/Nilson/Nielson children born to Nels and Sigrid or Nels and Kristine or Nels and Oline/Alice in appropriate respective timeframes (images 206 through 215; also looked through subsequent images to see if there were any from 1888-1894)	"Serine Elizabeth Nelsen" on 23 Sept 1882 th Nils and Kristine (name of child clearly written in later); Allert included (but no correction later--probably because no Social Security); NO CLARENCE

My research log tracks the date, description, purpose, and result of each search.

The goal of a research log is to track every search you conduct and to record the results. In the past, many genealogists used paper research logs with mixed results. You might start out researching Severina Larson, but your results might lead you to investigate a Serene Larson (who turns out to be unrelated), a Severina Jorgenson (who turns out to be your Severina, with a first husband's name), and a Sigrid Nelson (who turns out to be Severina's half-sister). If all of this is on a paper form, does it all go under Severina? How do you cross-reference items? How will you remember where you logged each search?

Because Evernote is so searchable, this problem is eliminated. You could put every single search you ever did into a single log, and you'd be able to find every bit of it again. Alternatively, you could have a research log for each family line, each ancestral location, each repository, or any other breakdown that makes sense to you. If your research goes in an unexpected direction, it doesn't matter, because you can tag it (or just search for it later).

Although you can customize your own research log to have whatever information or format you want, it's usually helpful to see a real-life example to think about how you want to set yours up. Here's what I include in my research log (see image).

- **Date:** This column contains the day and year I conducted the research.
- **Call Number:** This might include an actual library call number (for work done at a library or for interlibrary loan requests). If you're working with microfilm you

ordered from the Family History Library, this would be the film number (so you can search and see if you've already ordered that film). In the sample shown here, I was working online on FamilySearch.org, so there was no call number.

- **Description of Source:** Be as specific as possible. If you're on a website such as FamilySearch.org **<www.familysearch.org>** or Ancestry.com **<www.ancestry.com>**, record exactly what database or record set you're using so you're able to find it again online (and so you're able to avoid wasting time searching that same collection again). In my sample, you can see I have a full "bread crumb trail" for the resources I searched.

- **Purpose of Search:** Include every bit of search criteria you used. That way, if you come back days later and say to yourself, "I searched for Bill, Bob, Becky, Barbara, and Bonnie, but did I look for the half-brother Bud?" you'll know—because it's in your research log. If you have names that are commonly spelled wrong, it's especially important to record what variants you looked for. If you discover a new variant later, you can tell at a glance if you've already searched for that one or not.

- **Results:** Again, be specific. What do you want your future self to know about what you found here? Your future self will thank you for being as precise as possible.

Creating a Pull List

When I'm doing on-site research, I need to be as efficient as possible. As a working mom with two small kids, I don't get much time to hang out in repositories, so when I do, I want to make the most of every minute. That's why I create a list of exactly what records I need to pull before I ever leave home. Evernote is great for this, because it'll automatically sync to my mobile devices. That means I don't have to lug my computer around, because I have everything I need on my smartphone and tablet.

Pull lists are also great as de facto research logs. Since you've already entered the details about each record and what you hope to find on it, all you need to do is include the results. That makes it faster and easier to get to the part where you actually look for ancestors (and of course, that's the part we love best).

The contents of my pull list vary, based on what I'm looking for. If I'm working with newspaper records, for example, I'll create one where the date is the primary item, since newspaper microfilm rolls are usually housed in date order. For a visit to a Family History Library (see image **D**), I might include the film number first so I can sort those in numerical order (and avoid wandering around the stacks collecting films from different locations). If I'm traveling out of town to a repository, I'll use a tag to cross-reference my pull list with my other travel records (like my airline itinerary and hotel confirmation) so that I have all of my trip information in one place. You can create a new pull list for each trip that's customized for what you're looking for, or use a standard form for each trip.

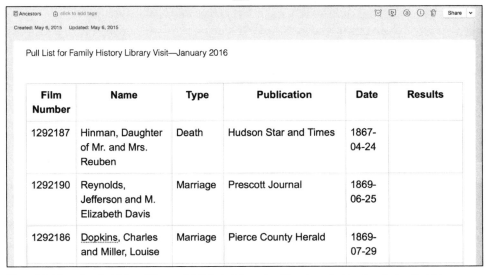

Pull List for Family History Library Visit—January 2016

Film Number	Name	Type	Publication	Date	Results
1292187	Hinman, Daughter of Mr. and Mrs. Reuben	Death	Hudson Star and Times	1867-04-24	
1292190	Reynolds, Jefferson and M. Elizabeth Davis	Marriage	Prescott Journal	1869-06-25	
1292186	Dopkins, Charles and Miller, Louise	Marriage	Pierce County Herald	1869-07-29	

My pull list for a Family History Library visit listed all the microfilms I wanted to view during that trip.

Creating a Census Abstract Form

Back in the olden days (that is, before the Internet), transcribing census records was one of the first tasks a new genealogist learned to do. You found your family in the Soundex microfilm (a phonetic last-name index to censuses), then you used that index record to find them in the census microfilm. You took a blank form, and you copied the information down.

Times have changed, and we can now download images from the census from home. In spite of that, many genealogists continue to transcribe their census records. Why?

- Transcribed records are easier to read. When you're working on a particular family, it's nice to be able to see all of their census records at a glance, without squinting or trying to decipher old handwriting.

- Transcribing helps you see important details. The act of writing (or typing) out the information helps you absorb it. I have census records I've looked at a dozen times, but when I copy that information down, I find that I notice clues I missed before. Looking is a passive act; transcribing is active. It makes a big difference in how much of the information you actually take in.

- Transcribed records (at least those in Evernote) are searchable. We can use Ancestry.com and other websites to look people up by name, but those sites don't provide a way to search all of our census records to see, for instance, how many of our ancestors

Name	Scott, William D	Mary	Margaret	Marie	Samuel	Lawrence	Isabel
Relationship	Self	Wife	Daughter	Daughter	Son	Son	Daughter
Owned/Rented	Owned						
Free or Mortgage	Free						
Sex	Male	Female	Female	Female	Male	Male	Male
Color/Race	White	White	White	White	White	White	White
Age	58	42	20	18	17	14	12
Martial Status	Married	Married	Single	Single	Single	Single	Single
Year of Immigration		1881					
Naturalized or Alien		Nat.					
Year of		1899					

When transcribing census records in Evernote, putting the headers down the side and the people across the top gives you more room.

were farmers or electricians. Being able to search every bit of data we have allows us to look at the information in different ways, and that helps us see patterns that can break down brick walls. If three people living on the same street were railroad workers, they probably knew each other. They might have even been brothers-in-law.

One of the first things you'll notice when you try to create a census extraction form in Evernote: The width is a huge problem. We're accustomed to having the various input fields go across the top horizontally and the names and information for the people vertically—because that's how the original census pages were designed. The maximum width of an Evernote table, though, is thirty columns. And if you actually set up a table with thirty columns, you'll find that they're so narrow they're tough to use.

The solution is easy: Turn that census form on its side (see image **E**).

Putting the headers down the left side and the people across the page gives you far more room to maneuver. This way, you can include every census field, even with longer censuses such as the 1940 Federal Census. You'll end up with a record you can tag for multiple people, occupations, locations, countries of origin, naturalization status—whatever you like. Appendix B has a list of all of the categories you'll need for each federal census from 1790 to 1940. If you're lucky enough to have ancestors who lived in states where state census records are available, don't forget to create forms for those, too.

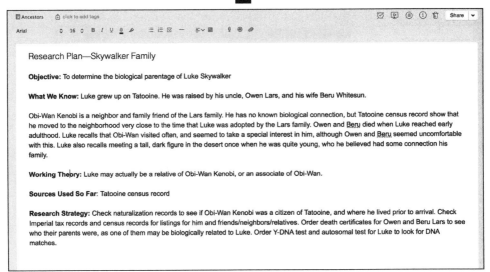

Your research plan should include these five essential components.

CREATING RESEARCH PLANS

Research plans can keep you on track and help you get more done. They allow you to zero in on a specific research question so you can identify possible sources of the answers to that question. This method can help keep you from the shotgun approach that leads to hours of Internet research but no concrete answers.

The key is making your research plan as useful as possible by following some best practices. A good research plan has at least five components (see image **F**):

1. A **stated objective** helps you zero in on the problem at hand. "Who are Luke Skywalker's parents?" is far more useful than "I want to know everything about Luke Skywalker."

2. A **list of facts** you already have (and where the information came from) is essential. This spells out what you have so you can focus on what you don't have.

3. A **working theory** gives you direction. You might be wrong, but your best guess is often a great starting point.

4. A **list of sources** you've already consulted saves time. You want to spend your time and energy on new resources, not revisiting old records.

5. A **research strategy** is where you outline what you'll do next. Spelling this out can really help clarify your thinking and allow you to move forward. No more wandering aimlessly all over the Internet; once you have a plan, you can execute that plan. That leads to results.

Putting all these components in Evernote ensures that you can find your notes again and track your progress over time. Having your research plan available on multiple devices means you can use whatever bits of time you have to work on the problem, without having to scramble around to find your notes.

INDEXING RECORDS INSTANTLY

One of my favorite aspects of Evernote is the indexing. I have roots in areas where no newspapers are available online (yet), so I still have to order newspaper microfilms through interlibrary loan, then manually read each one of them to find my ancestors. It's fascinating, but it's not fast.

My local library has modern microfilm readers that allow me to save images of newspapers to a flash drive, but I no longer use them. That's because I found that it took too long to save the image to the flash drive. Worse, when I *did* save those articles to a flash drive, I had no way of recording the source citation. I was keeping a manual list of image names and carefully writing out the date, page number, and column number of each article. It was a mess.

When I discovered that I could take photos in Evernote (image **G**) and record the citations right under the photos, I was amazed. Then I figured out that I could search on every word of that article in the image itself—and I was blown away. My productivity soared.

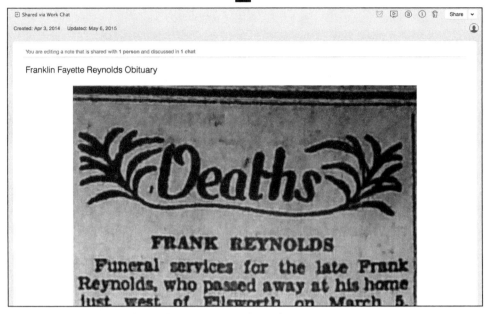

I captured this obituary by taking a photo of the microfilm reader screen. I typed the source citation below the image and moved on. Evernote indexed the obituary, so I can find it by searching for any word (including the names of the deceased's survivors, his employer, his place of birth, or anything else that appears).

Before Evernote, it took me about eleven hours to get through a year's worth of weekly newspapers in the town I was working on. I can get through that same year's worth in just under six hours now.

You can easily do the same. Let's review how to take a photo of a document in Evernote:

1. Open the Evernote app on your tablet or smartphone, then click the Camera icon. It's the second icon from the left on the Evernote app.

2. Aim at the document you need to capture, allow the autofocus to operate for a second or two, then take the photo. Evernote will automatically detect the fact that you're photographing a document. When I'm working with microfilm, I take a photo of the screen itself (on the newer microfilm readers that work on a computer screen) or the image surface (on the older, manual microfilm readers). The surface of older readers is slanted, so it takes some practice to get a good photo.

3. Once you've taken the photo, a checkmark appears in the lower right corner of the screen. Click it.

4. Click the link titled Snapshot at the top of the Notes list. The snapshot you took most recently will always be at the top of the list.

INBOX   click to add tags

Created: May 6, 2015   Updated: May 6, 2015

Share ▾

New Mexico Genealogist March 2015: Vol. 54, No. 1

NEW MEXICO GENEALOGIST

VOL. 54, NO. 1 MARCH 2015

Contents

Articles

A Brief Genealogy of New Mexico Governor Antonio Narbona... 3
        by Rick Hendricks and Robert D. Martínez

Generations of Service.. 10
        by Benito Eloy Romero

I took a photo in Evernote of this genealogical journal's table of contents. Now I'll be able to search my Evernote files for the name of the author or a word in the article, and instantly figure out what issue to pull off my bookshelf.

5. You'll see the photo you just took. Check to be sure the document isn't too blurry, then tap underneath it and type in your source citation. Be sure to add a title to your note by clicking next to the word *Snapshot* at the top, then typing your preferred title over it. When you're done, click the elephant in the top left corner to go back to the main screen.

One underappreciated use for this feature is creating an index of your books and periodicals. Denise Barrett Olson of the Moultrie Creek Gazette **<moultriecreek.us/gazette>** recommends taking a photo of the table of contents of your journals and other print material (image **H**). This creates an instant index so you can search your Evernote records to find out what articles you have on a particular topic.

You can do this with old family histories as well (image **I**). I inherited one from my husband's family, written in 1929, and it sat in a drawer for years while I had the best of intentions to transcribe and index it. Evernote did the job in seconds.

GEOTAGGING IMPORTANT FAMILY SITES

Evernote allows you to add a location to any note. This is helpful for many genealogical uses, including the items on the following list:

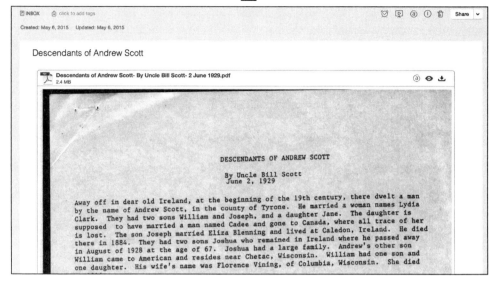

If you have old family histories compiled by genealogists from generations ago, get those images into Evernote and take advantage of the syncing, automatic backups, and indexing.

- locating the family farm or home;
- locating graves (especially those in rural areas that may be off the beaten path—or off the map altogether);
- tracking DNA cousins (more on this in the next section); and
- tracking the place of origin of immigrants who settled in a particular area, to spot clues indicating which people may have come to the new place together (and therefore may have been kin back in the old location).

You can probably think of other uses based on your genealogy needs. To set a location for a note in Evernote, follow these steps (illustrated on image **J**):

1. Open the note you want to work with.

2. Look for the Information icon (it's the circled letter-i icon in the top right corner). Click it, and a pop-up menu will appear.

3. One of the fields you can enter is Location. Enter your location, then hit Enter.

This allows you to click the Atlas link (image **K**), which will show your notes by location. You'll be able to see your notes actually plotted out on a map (image **L**). That's a powerful tool when you're going to visit your ancestor's hometown and want to see where stuff is located. When you visit the actual locations, you can just click on the note to view the relevant items for that spot.

You can add a location to a note, such as the cemetery and town where this headstone is located.

Notes

Notebooks

Tags

Atlas

Market

Announcements

The Atlas option is in the navigation menu on the left side of your screen.

Using the Atlas link will plot your geotagged notes on a map.

TRACKING YOUR DNA RESULTS

DNA is the shiny new plaything of many genealogists. It's great fun to do DNA testing, but the first time you get your results of an autosomal DNA test, it's a bit overwhelming: Suddenly you have thousands of new cousins, all with surnames you don't recognize. Often they have ethnicities you don't recognize either. Somehow you have to wade through your family trees to figure out where the connections are. Many genealogists find that it's a lot like untangling Christmas lights, and some even throw up their hands and give up.

Evernote is a huge help in making sense of it all. Here are some ideas for how to use Evernote to figure out how you're connected to all those new cousins:

- Your autosomal DNA results will list the degree of relationship between you and your matches—second cousin, fourth cousin, and so on. Make a list of your fifty closest cousins, and use the geotagging feature (see the previous section) to tag the locations where their ancestors lived. This can really help you spot patterns.

- Make a separate note for each of your chromosomes. Track who matches you on each chromosome and where specifically on the chromosome they match (see image **M**). Both 23andMe **<www.23andme.com>** and Family Tree DNA **<www.familytreedna. com>** offer chromosome browsers that help you do this. AncestryDNA currently does not offer this feature, but you can get around that by taking your AncestryDNA results and uploading them to a free utility called GEDmatch **<www.gedmatch.com>**. This will allow you to see exactly where you match each AncestryDNA cousin. Using this technique, I discovered that a large chunk of my chromosome 9 came from a particular set of fourth great-grandparents, which helped me determine how each of my matches on chromosome 9 was related to that couple. Over time, you'll figure out the origins of more and more sections of your DNA, which is what you need in order to see how those cousins are connected.

- Track your GEDmatch cousin kit numbers. If you're like most genealogists, you'll end up managing a number of DNA kits for a variety of your nongenealogist relatives. If you use GEDmatch, each one of those will be assigned a unique kit number. You'll want to keep track of

POWER-USER TIP

Demystify DNA Testing

Does genetic genealogy make your head spin? Wondering what test you should take, or how to make sense of your results? Family Tree University offers several courses on genetic genealogy with an expert instructor to provide guidance and answer your questions. Its Virtual Conferences also offer a DNA education track. See **<www.familytreeuniversity. com>** for details.

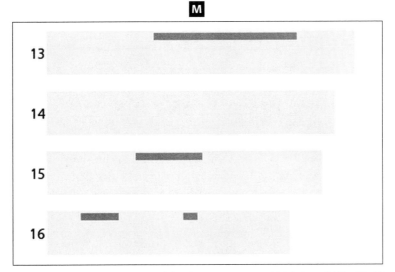

I'm using Evernote to keep track of the chromosomes on which I share DNA with this second cousin twice removed. Then, when I find new cousins who match me on those same segments, I can dig deeper to see if they might be related on the same line.

those so you can use them to run reports against new matches. For example, if I have a new third cousin match, I'll want to run that person's GEDmatch number against those of my other known cousins. That way, I can determine which of them match this new person, which tells me how we might be related.

- Use the AncestryDNA tool developed by Jeff Snavely to create a list of your cousin matches and store it in Evernote for easy reference and searching. This tool is a Google Chrome web browser extension that allows you to download a list of your AncestryDNA matches. It also downloads the names of ancestors in any public trees of your matches. That allows you to see which names appear in multiple matches' trees, which can point to common ancestors. To get this extension, you first need to have Chrome installed (it's a free download from **<www.google.com/intl/en/ chrome>**). Open Chrome, then go to **<chrome.google.com/webstore>** and search on AncestryDNA Helper. Click the Free button to add it to Chrome.

- Keep notes about your adoptee cousins. It's inevitable that you'll have some cousin matches who don't know who their parents are because of adoption, nonpaternity events, or other unknown parentage situations. In those cases, you'll want to have a place to track clues that they have so you can match them over time against information that comes in later. I had an adoptee cousin who had very few clues when we first matched in 2011, but over time, we found bits and pieces of information, mostly from new DNA cousins who turned up. Tracking every bit of it in Evernote helped us finally spot the pattern that led to solving her case. Searches like these are often a marathon rather than a sprint, so it's especially important to keep everything in a central, searchable location.

CATALOGING FAMILY HEIRLOOMS

I have a cup that was brought over from Germany by my third great-grandmother in the late 1840s or early 1850s. Here's the problem: I have two German third great-grandmothers. Nobody wrote down which one of them owned this cup, and now that fact is lost to history.

This is why I'm taking photos of every family heirloom I have and detailing which ancestors they came from. When possible, I include a photo of the ancestor as well (see images **N** and **O**). This ensures that my kids will know exactly where all of our family heirlooms came from. I've found that involving my kids in this process also gets them interested in family history, which is a real bonus. I let my nine-year-old use the Evernote camera to take the photo, then I type in notes about the person and the item.

N

My daughter took this photo of her great-great-grandmother Sara Johnston and the afghan Sara made. Sara is now her favorite ancestor, and no one will wonder where the afghan came from.

We have only one piece of letterhead from the lumber mill run by my husband's great-grandfather. We've preserved it (along with his photo) via Evernote.

RECORDING YOUR OWN HISTORY

In chapter 6, we talked about how to use Evernote's audio recording feature to conduct interviews with family members. That's a great use of the recording feature, but what about you? Have you recorded your own family stories? Genealogists are often like the shoemaker's children who go barefoot: We dig and dig for our ancestors' stories, but we don't put as much effort into our own. Sitting down to write your own family history can feel like a daunting task, but talking might be much easier. Consider spending five minutes a day creating an audio note with tidbits about your own life. You'll be leaving behind a priceless gift for your descendants (and it will be in your own voice).

Audio files are also a fun way to capture your kids' or grandkids' growth. Set your smartphone out and start talking. In fact, talk to your kids about their ancestors, and let them ask questions. Think how excited you'd be to have a recording of your grandparents

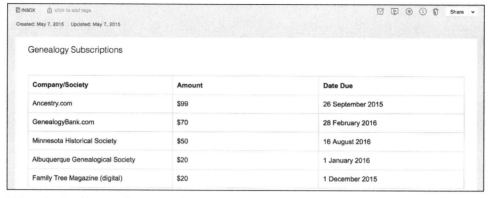

Genealogy Subscriptions

Company/Society	Amount	Date Due
Ancestry.com	$99	26 September 2015
GenealogyBank.com	$70	28 February 2016
Minnesota Historical Society	$50	16 August 2016
Albuquerque Genealogical Society	$20	1 January 2016
Family Tree Magazine (digital)	$20	1 December 2015

Make a simple table to track your genealogy subscriptions and memberships.

talking to *their* grandparents about the old days. We can't make that happen, but we can leave that gift behind for those who come after us.

TRACKING GENEALOGICAL SUBSCRIPTIONS AND MEMBERSHIPS

It seems like the more involved we get in family history, the more subscriptions we have to track. From websites to magazines to society memberships, it can be hard to remember what bills are coming due. For websites, it's especially important to stay on top of subscriptions, since some of them will auto-renew unless we take steps to cancel them (and we aren't always notified). Create a note in Evernote that includes the renewal date and amount so you can stay on top of your budget (see image). You can even add a reminder so you know when you decide whether to renew (learn more about setting reminders in chapter 6).

KEEPING TRACK OF IDEAS

Ever had a great idea on where to look for an elusive ancestor? It would be nice if this sort of inspiration struck while you were in front of your computer, working on your research. Alas, that rarely happens. Instead, those bolts of lightning often hit when you're folding laundry, watering the flowers, or walking through the home improvement store.

If you have Evernote on your smartphone, though, that's not a problem. You can create a note called Ideas, then add those clues in (see image **Q**). Put in a reminder for a time you're more likely to be at your desk, and you're all set. Now those great ideas are never lost, and you don't have to waste brainpower trying to remember them.

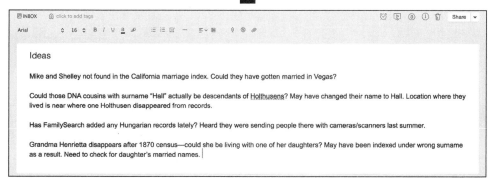

Evernote provides a convenient place to store those random ideas that come at the most inconvenient times. Set reminders so you don't forget to follow up.

MAKING CONFERENCES MORE VALUABLE

If you've attended a genealogy conference recently, you may have noticed that fewer people are walking around hunched over like they're lugging around a heavy weight. That's because more and more genealogists are choosing to receive the conference syllabus electronically before the conference starts. This allows them to store it in Evernote and to annotate and make notes so they can get the most out of their conference experience. That syllabus will be searchable (for Premium users), and it won't sit on the bookshelf collecting dust (or worse, be left behind in the hotel room because it was too heavy for the suitcase).

If you attend virtual conferences (such as Family Tree University's Virtual Conference), you'll often have lots of downloaded materials. Evernote is a great place to store those so you can find them again when you have the time to begin to apply what you've learned.

CREATING A READING LIST

The Internet is wonderful. We're lucky to live in a time when we have information on every conceivable topic at our fingertips. That said, if you sometimes feel a bit overwhelmed by the sheer volume of information coming at you every day, you're not alone. In the space of a lunch hour, you can come across dozens of blog posts, articles, infographics, tutorials, and charts you truly want to read. The problem is finding the time.

One solution is to store all of these items in Evernote. Then, when you're waiting at the dentist's office or stuck in line at the drive-thru, you can pull out your smartphone or tablet and start reading. You won't get quite as much time to play Bejeweled this way, but you'll come out a lot smarter.

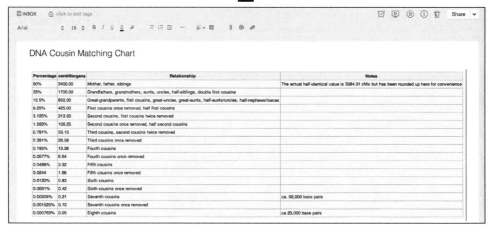

I keep this DNA cousin-matching chart from the International Society of Genetic Genealogy handy by storing it in Evernote. It allows me to see at a glance how closely related a new match might be.

This method is especially helpful when you're learning about DNA and genetic genealogy. Most people find this topic daunting at first, and it often takes quite some time for all of the concepts to sink in. It tends to be a process rather than an event, and it often happens as you begin to work with your own DNA results. Saving those handy DNA articles so you can revisit them as your understanding evolves can be helpful. There are also certain reference tools that you'll need constantly as you work with DNA results, and Evernote is a handy place to store those as well (see image **R**).

PLANNING FAMILY REUNIONS

Much of the process of planning a family reunion involves creating documents that end up being exactly the sort of thing a future genealogist would want. For example, you'll need a list of the family members, along with their addresses for mailing invitations. Wouldn't you love to have that list for your ancestors' reunion from 1890? Using Evernote to plan the reunion allows you to keep those documents without any extra effort. In fact, you could convert them to PDF files and send them out to every attendee so they're available to everyone.

The nuts and bolts of reunion planning are also well-suited to Evernote (see image **S**). You might need to buy hundreds of paper plates, cups, napkins, etc. What's the most cost-effective place to buy them? Go to a few big box or warehouse stores and take photos of the prices in your Evernote app. It's the fastest, easiest way to comparison shop. Thinking about buying new picnic tables for the backyard so everyone has a place to sit? Take photos of the prices and the tables so you can compare those, too.

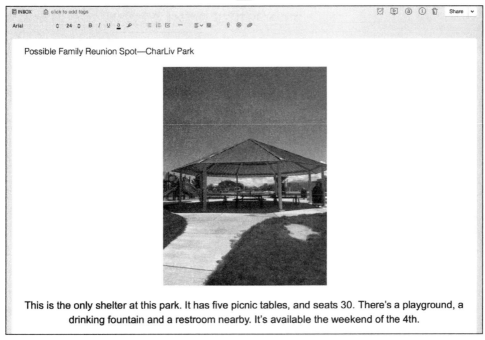

Possible Family Reunion Spot—CharLiv Park

This is the only shelter at this park. It has five picnic tables, and seats 30. There's a playground, a drinking fountain and a restroom nearby. It's available the weekend of the 4th.

Use Evernote to find a site for a family reunion and take photos of each one. You can use the Share feature to collaborate with your fellow reunion planners.

Don't forget to seize the opportunity to get those visiting relatives interested in family history. You can use Presentation Mode to show them some of your greatest finds since the last reunion, and use the audio recording feature to get them talking about what they remember about their own ancestors. You can learn more about how to use these features in chapter 6.

OTHER FAMILY HISTORY-RELATED IDEAS

Sometimes genealogists forget that the records we work with weren't actually created for genealogists at all. We treasure diaries, letters, cards, and other artifacts from everyday life.

We also tend to forget that we ourselves generate plenty of artifacts that our descendants might like to have one hundred years from now. One of my favorite family history items is a small baby book that my great-grandmother put together for her only son. My own children's baby books, however, are a half-finished pile of good intentions in a drawer in my office.

Using Evernote gives you an opportunity to remedy this. Because it's so easy to use, you can create records that make your own daily life easier. Even better, those notes can then be preserved without any extra effort on your part. Let's look at some ideas for records that you can use today, then pass on tomorrow.

Gift Lists

I'm one of those people who shops for the holidays year-round. I often see something that will make a perfect gift and tuck it away until it's needed. I save lots of money this way, but I sometimes forget what I have. I originally started using Evernote to keep an inventory of the presents I'd bought for each family member (image 🅣). Now, however, I realize that I have a record of my children's growth and changing interests. The little girl who wanted the Barbie Dream House in 2009 is now a big girl who wants a trip to gymnastics camp.

Menus for Big Events

If you entertain or have houseguests for family holidays, you probably put some time and effort into your menu planning. I'm glad I was using Evernote the year I started hosting Thanksgiving, because I've used it to plan my menus for years (see image 🅤). Now I have a complete list of everything served, including the results of new recipes I made and whether I had too much of one thing or not enough of another. That helped me host better meals over time, but it's also something that my great-grandchildren might enjoy reading. I convert the menu notes to PDF each year and save them for future generations.

Garden Planning

Depending on where you live, gardening might well be part of your family history. My grandpa was known for his tomato gardening, and my father-in-law grew the best asparagus I've ever eaten. My family's first home was eighty years old, and a woman who'd grown up there in the 1950s stopped by once and told us that her mother had planted the peonies that still thrived in our yard. Gardening can be a big connection to your roots.

I use Evernote to plan my garden and note what worked and what didn't, and I use the camera feature to take photos of the progress of the trees and bushes we've planted. We live in the desert, so I also track our water usage to see where we can make more conservation-friendly choices. All of this is part of my own family's history, which includes our move from the Midwest to New Mexico (and the adjustments we made as a result). It's like a mini diary of our experience, and I hope future generations will find it interesting.

Wedding Planning

If you're planning a wedding, there's no better tool than Evernote. From keeping track of your budget to creating a to-do list to storing photos of the dress, the venue, and the flowers, Evernote can do it all. The ability to share notebooks allows you to include others in the

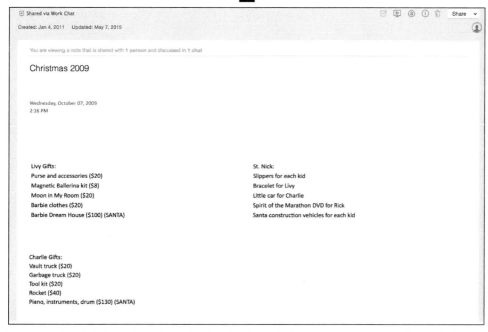

Keep your gift lists in Evernote to stay on track and under budget, and save them to see a slice of life for your family each year.

U

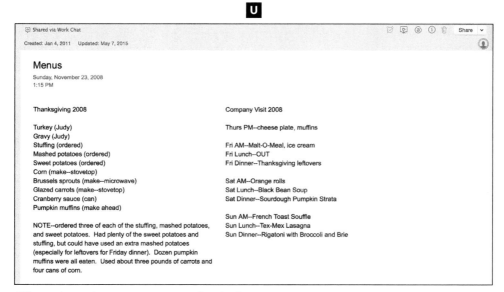

I'd love to know what my ancestors served at Thanksgiving. My descendants will have a detailed list (and an understanding of how popular mashed potatoes were in my family).

My great-grandmother saved this guest book from her wedding in 1913. We have the option of saving far more detail for our descendants.

planning process, even if they're far away. When you're done, you'll have a complete chronicle of the entire experience. You can even photograph the pages from the guest book at the big event (see image **V**), then store them in Evernote with the rest of the wedding stuff.

Baby Books and Kids' Schoolwork and Artwork

If you have kids or grandkids, you have stuff. Lots of stuff. Our offspring come home from the hospital with paperwork, and it grows from there. You might buy a baby book with the intention of putting it all in there. In fact, with the first child, you might even succeed. But subsequent children almost never have baby books, because parents of multiple small children just don't have the time to put them together.

Once the kids start school, there's even more stuff. They bring home art projects and little essays every day. You want to save it all, but who has the space?

If you have Evernote, you have the space. My elementary-school-age kids choose one piece of artwork or schoolwork per week, and they take the photo in Evernote themselves (see image **W**). This means they feel better about throwing out the other stuff because they choose the winner of week. I feel better about not having piles of construction paper proj-

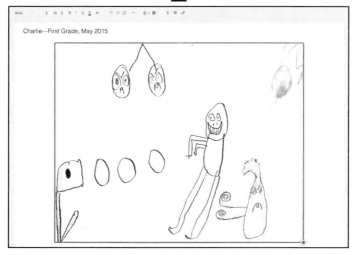

Charlie—First Grade, May 2015

I'm told this Plants v. Zombies picture done by my first-grader will be a collector's item in thirty years. Thank goodness we saved it in Evernote.

ects stuffed in every closet. We both win, and I'll have far more stuff saved to show their children someday. I also have audio files of each of them on the first day of school every year, telling me how their day went. It's a much more comprehensive picture of who they were at each stage than I could have achieved with an old-fashioned baby book (although you could certainly print the notes and turn them into a book, if you like).

Family Recipes

Nearly every family has some recipes or culinary traditions passed down from one generation to the next. Often these are either written on recipe cards (which can easily fall victim to kitchen mishaps), or they're not written down at all. Capture whatever you have in Evernote, so you can search, tag, and find those recipes again. You might find that you want to put all of your recipes in Evernote—not just the ones passed down from family members (image X). When you're out running errands at 4 P.M. and realize dinner is on the horizon, being able to pull up a recipe means you can buy the ingredients on the fly, rather than resorting to take-out food.

If you have relatives who are great cooks but never use a recipe, think about interviewing them using the Evernote audio recording feature. This way, you have a valuable recording of them explaining their methods in their own words. Later you can transcribe the recipe portion of the interview and distribute it to other family members. This way, recipes are no longer lost when your loved ones pass on.

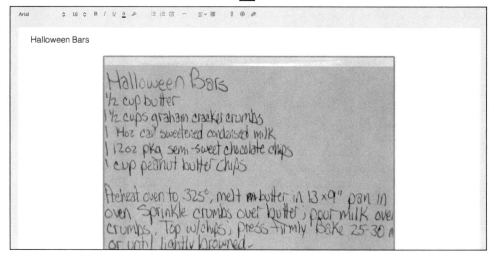

I'm in the process of taking Evernote photos of all of my old recipe cards. This one dates back to the mid-1980s. I can tag them with the name of the ancestor they came from, the type of cuisine, or even the occasion for which they're usually served.

USING EVERNOTE TO MAKE LIFE EASIER

One way to get really good at using Evernote is to use it every day. That means you'll need to go beyond family history to stuff that may not be worthy of saving but will make you more efficient in running your household. A more efficient household means more time for gene-alogy. That's a win-win. So let's talk about a few ideas for using Evernote regularly.

Grocery Lists

Once you've begun using Evernote to track your grocery list, you'll wonder how you lived without it. Because it syncs across devices, and because notes are sharable, you can ensure that the other adults in your household can access a complete, up-to-date list at all times. That means there's always the possibility that someone else will do the grocery shopping for you.

If you're on the iOS platform, check out an app called Grocerytrip **<www.hcrisp.com/ grocerytrip>**. It takes your random, unsorted grocery list from Evernote and puts it into neat sections that correspond to the aisles of most grocery stores. It's a great time-saver.

Home Improvement Projects

If you're making improvements to your home, track them in Evernote. This allows you to easily construct a complete list of improvements made during your time there, which can help considerably when it's time to sell your home. You also can track paint colors, carpet types, and other tough-to-remember details. Keep information on what size furnace filter you need and what type of bags your vacuum cleaner uses, so you can pick them up when you're shopping (and track prices so you know if that good deal is actually a good deal). Track when you last handled routine maintenance such as cleaning the gutters or cleaning the back of the refrigerator, and set reminders so you know when it's time to do them again. If you install items that might make you eligible for a tax break, such as energy-efficient windows, be sure to tag them so you can find them again at tax time.

Book Inventory Tracking

Most genealogists love books, and we buy them every chance we get. Past a certain point, though, it can be tough to remember what you already have. Keeping a list of your book inventory in Evernote means that you'll always have this information on your smartphone or tablet so you can double-check it before you buy.

This is especially handy when buying books for nieces, nephews, and grandchildren. It's hard to remember what Nancy Drew books you bought two years ago, which is a problem when you go to buy more. Keep a list of what you've given and you'll never have to rack your brain to remember.

You can also use Evernote to record books you've read and books you plan to read. If you're a member of a book club, you can keep your notes in Evernote so you have them with you wherever you're reading.

KEYS to SUCCESS

✳ Maximize Evernote's usefulness by using it as much as possible. Keeping everything genealogy-related in one place gives you the ability to cross-reference, and it ensures that your important data are backed up and always available on all of your devices.

✳ Use Evernote to help you build and maintain good research habits. Create a correspondence log and a research log, and commit to using them regularly.

✳ Harness the power of Evernote's ability to index text in images by taking photos of anything you want to be able to search.

✳ Remember to preserve your own family history while pursuing your ancestors. You and your family will be sought-after relatives in records some day. You can use Evernote to build a legacy of your own life.

✳ Think about ways to use Evernote in your daily life. This will make you more proficient at using Evernote, and it will make your life easier so you have more time for genealogy.

Syncing and Securing Your Evernote Data on Mobile Devices

I was at a grocery store in Albuquerque a few months ago when I spotted her. She was reaching over the bananas, wearing an old T-shirt that said "Albert Lea High School." I walked over and asked, "Hey, is that Albert Lea, Minnesota?"

It was. My great-grandmother came from Albert Lea, and hers did, too. I pulled out my phone and opened Evernote, and showed her some photos I'd just web-clipped from an Albert Lea High School yearbook from the early 1900s. It turned out that one of her ancestors was pictured on the same page as mine.

This is one of the many reasons I love Evernote. Because it runs on every one of my devices, I always have it with me, no matter what I'm doing. I don't have to plan ahead because it's all in my pocket, all the time. I wouldn't have guessed that I'd have a genealogical research opportunity in the produce department of my grocery store, but thanks to Evernote, I was ready when serendipity struck.

Evernote works on a wide variety of platforms. In fact, it's hard to think of another app that's so versatile. You can use Evernote on

- iOS devices, such as iPhone, iPad, and iPod Touch;
- Android devices, such as Google Nexus, Amazon Kindle Fire, and Samsung Galaxy;

A

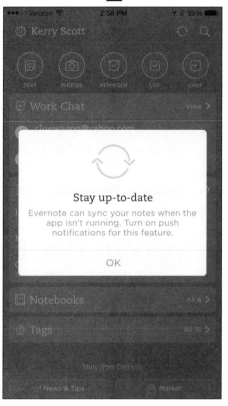

B

This is one of the few mobile devices that won't work with Evernote.

Allowing your Evernote app to sync even when you're not using it ensures that your notes will always be available when you need them.

- Windows devices, such as Surface Pro and Nokia Lumia; and
- BlackBerry devices, such as PlayBook and Passport.

This means that if you bought your device within the past few years (unlike image **A**), Evernote will probably work with it. Your devices don't need to be on the same platform, either. You can mix it up by using, say, a MacBook Air with a Samsung Galaxy tablet and a BlackBerry Passport phone. Evernote doesn't mind if you're not wedded to one particular brand or operating system.

SYNCING YOUR DATA

If you're looking to add your mobile devices into your Evernote experience, your first concern is probably how to get the data on your device. Fortunately, that's easy. Once you've installed the app on your device, open it up. You'll be prompted to enter your username and password. After you log on, things will look disturbingly bleak for a minute or two (depending on your connection speed and the amount of data you have in Evernote). Once the sync is complete, all of your notes, notebooks, and stacks will appear.

Push or Manual Sync?

Depending on your device, you'll likely see a pop-up message the first time you log on, asking if you'd like Evernote to sync your notes even when you're not actively running the Evernote app on your device (image **B**). I like having this option, and I've found that the difference in battery life is negligible, even on my older devices (although BlackBerry devices tend to be the exception to this rule). If you opt not to do this, you'll need to manually sync your notes by tapping the Sync icon (the circle with arrows in it) in the upper right part of the screen. It will spin while it syncs and stop when it's done. If you don't get the pop-up message asking about this, go into your device's Notifications settings to set it manually.

Keep in mind that you'll want to sync often if you choose to do so manually. There's nothing worse than needing a bit of data and realizing you don't have a strong enough signal to sync. It's also a good idea to plan to sync when you have access to Wi-Fi so you don't use up the bandwidth allowance on your cell phone plan. Those photos, audio files, and other big items in your notes can really take a bite out of your monthly data plan.

Limiting Synchronization

As you use Evernote more and more, you'll find that you use it for more than just genealogy. When that happens, you might end up creating notes or notebooks that you don't want to sync across devices. For example, if you're storing your income tax information in a particular notebook, it might make sense to keep that on your desktop computer alone. You might lose your phone someday, but you're somewhat less likely to lose your desktop computer.

When you create a new notebook, by default, it will be set up to sync with the Evernote servers (and therefore with all of your devices). Unfortunately, as of this writing, that

Sync on Wi-Fi Only

If you're not yet at the end of the month and you're running out of bandwidth on your data plan, one option is to set your Evernote mobile version to synchronize only on Wi-Fi. I've often found that when I'm on a research trip, I take a lot of photos in Evernote, and those uploads during the sync process can push me close to my data plan's limits. To change this setting, open Evernote, tap the gear in the upper left corner to open Settings, then tap General. Move the slider for Synchronize on Wi-Fi Only to toggle this setting.

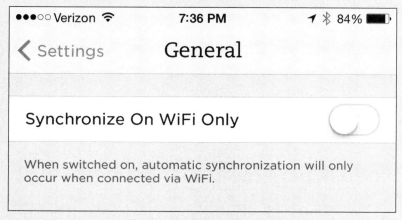

This little-known setting can save you from expensive data overage fees on your mobile phone bill.

option can't be changed once the notebook has been created. For that reason, it's important to follow this process to create a local notebook (that is, one stored locally and not synced):

1. From your desktop or laptop computer, choose File from the top menu, then New Notebook. You'll see that you have the option to create either a Synchronized Notebook or a Local Notebook (image **C**).

2. Choose Local Notebook, then type in the name you want to use.

Remember that a local notebook is just that—local. Because it's not synchronized with the Evernote servers, it's not backed up in the cloud like the rest of your Evernote content. Be sure to back up manually on a regular basis to ensure you don't lose your data. You can learn more about how to do this in chapter 11.

You'll need to follow specific steps to create a notebook that doesn't sync with the Evernote cloud.

KEEPING YOUR DATA LOCKED DOWN

It's pretty easy to keep your data secure when they're in your house, on your desktop computer. You set a password to log in to your computer, lock your doors when you leave your house, and that's it. Once you and your devices are out in the wild, though, things can get dicey.

Many of us have the best of intentions when it comes to keeping our devices secure. We've heard the advice about setting a passcode, and we mean to do that—someday. But the ease of grabbing our phone or tablet and getting started with it often wins out. That's not necessarily a problem for many of the apps on your phone; it's unlikely that thieves are itching to get at your weather app or to play Angry Birds. When it comes to your Evernote files, though, it's not a bad idea to lock them down, away from prying eyes or practical jokers.

Evernote Plus and Premium subscribers have the option of setting a passcode on both iOS and Evernote devices. As of this writing, that function isn't available on BlackBerry or Windows devices, and it isn't an option for users of the Basic (free) version of Evernote (although it's possible it will be soon, as this is a sore spot with many Evernote Basic users). Here's how to lock down your iOS device:

On an iPhone, set a passcode lock from this screen.

1. Open Evernote on your iPhone, iPad, or iPod touch.

2. Tap the gear icon in the upper left corner to open the Settings dialog screen.

3. Tap Premium. It's the second option on the list.

4. Tap Passcode Lock. This one is also the second option on the list.

5. Tap Turn Passcode On (image **D**). Enter a four-digit passcode.

6. If you like, you can change the setting for how fast your phone requires a passcode. The default setting is Immediately, but you can set it to prompt for a password after anywhere from one minute to four hours of idle time.

You can set up an Evernote passcode on your Android phone or tablet, too. Here's how to secure your Android device:

1. Open Evernote on your phone or tablet.

2. Tap Menu, then tap Settings.

3. Tap Setup PIN Lock. Enter a four-digit passcode.

✳ Install Evernote on every device you own. This ensures that you always have your data available. You'll be amazed at how often it comes in handy.

✳ Choose the sync option that best meets your needs. In most cases, automatic syncing is a good choice because it allows you to set it and forget it. If you're concerned about going over your data plan or maintaining your battery life (especially while on the road), a manual sync or syncing only over Wi-Fi might be a better option.

✳ If you have data you don't want on your phone or tablet, you can still use Evernote on those devices. Just set up your notebook so that it's stored locally on your computer and excluded from syncing activities.

✳ Consider choosing a passcode lock for your Evernote app so people who have your device can't access your data without your permission.

EVERNOTE SYNCING AND SECURING CHECKLIST

☐ Download Evernote to each of your devices. See chapter 2 for help with installation and setup.

☐ Decide whether you want to sync your data manually or automatically

    ☐ Manually

    ☐ Automatically

☐ You can adjust this in your mobile device's Notifications setting or in the Preferences settings of the desktop software. The web version of Evernote syncs automatically.

☐ Set a passcode on your mobile Evernote apps (for Premium subscribers on iOS and Android) for added security.

    ☐ Passcode: _____

☐ For any data you don't wish to sync—such as confidential financial information—create those notes within a local notebook.

Data Not to Sync	Saved to Local Notebook?

Enhancing Evernote with External Tools

Evernote is a great product all by itself. One of its best qualities, though, is its ability to play nice with others. A variety of companies have designed products and apps that will enhance your Evernote experience. Some of these were developed in partnership with Evernote, while others are freestanding products. All of them will help you get the most out of your Evernote experience.

In this chapter, we'll explore some of the top Evernote add-ons to enhance your genealogy work. Some are physical items ideal for people who still prefer taking notes on paper; others are apps designed to work with mobile versions of Evernote. All apps listed here are free. You'll find even more add-ons in the Evernote App Center **<appcenter.evernote.com>**.

PENULTIMATE

Penultimate (image **A**) is my absolute favorite Evernote tool. This iPad app allows you to handwrite notes or create drawings and have them integrate seamlessly into your Evernote files. Although Evernote says that your handwritten Penultimate notes are searchable, my own experience is that this varies widely with the quality of your handwriting.

Penultimate works seamlessly with Evernote.

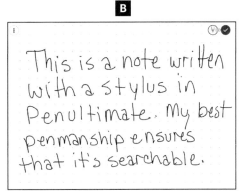

You can handwrite notes that are searchable in Evernote.

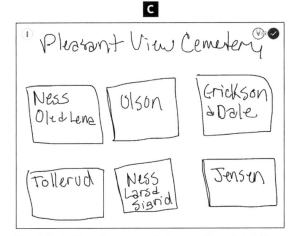

People buried together in cemeteries are often related. You can sketch this out in Penultimate right in the cemetery, then take photos of the headstones using the Evernote camera. You'll have all of the information you need in one place.

When I make a concerted effort to print clearly, I usually can search my notes (image **B**), but my regular handwriting typically doesn't work (admittedly, my regular handwriting would make a first-grade teacher cry).

I've used Penultimate to take notes in genealogy classes, to sketch out a quick family tree on the fly, and to draw a rudimentary map to a remote cemetery and farm (image **C**). Of course, you can tag your Penultimate notes to make them easier to find, and you can move them around and add them to existing notebooks. They'll sync with the desktop version of Evernote, where you can manage them as you would any other note.

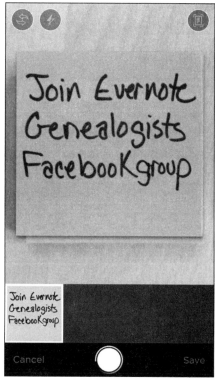

Choosing a Stylus

If you use Penultimate (or any other handwriting-to-Evernote app), you'll need to buy a stylus to write with. A stylus is like a pen, but with a special soft tip that doesn't scratch your tablet. Prices range from around $5 to over $100. Generally speaking, the thinner the tip, the more the stylus costs. It's a good idea to try out a few different types of stylus to see what type you prefer before you commit to an expensive one. I tried several (including the $74.95 Jot Script 2 sold by Evernote **<www.evernote.com/market/feature/jotscript2-stylus-iOS>**) and found that my favorite was one that costs $10. Shop for a stylus on Amazon **<www.amazon.com>**, or if you want to see your options in person, try Best Buy or an office supply store.

Take a photo of a Post-it Note, and Evernote will keep it for you—and even file it based on the color of the paper if you so choose.

There's no freestanding version of Penultimate for Android devices, but the Android version of Evernote itself incorporates many of its features. That's because Evernote bought Penultimate in 2012 and worked hard to integrate those features into the Android offering. To get the app for iPad, search for *Penultimate* in the Apple App Store

POST-IT NOTES

Evernote has a special relationship with 3M, the company that makes Post-it Notes. You can use the built-in Evernote camera to take photos of Post-It Notes, and Evernote will automatically detect the image is a Post-It Note and file it accordingly. You can designate certain colors of Post-It Notes for certain notebooks or tags (say, green for genealogy, blue for household, pink for shopping lists), and Evernote will autodetect the color and put your note in the right place (image **D**). As always, your handwritten notes are searchable.

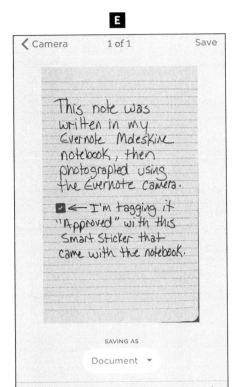

Evernote Moleskin notebooks come with Smart Stickers, which you can use to tag your notes automatically when you take photos using the Evernote camera.

The Moleskine Smart Stickers include tags for Home, Action, Rejected, Approved, Travel, and Work.

You don't even need a steady hand to take the photo; if it's crooked, Evernote will auto-straighten it for you. If you have a bunch of Post-it Notes, you can take the photos all at once and Evernote will automatically put them into a notebook just for Post-it Notes, so you can sort them out at your leisure (or just leave them there). You can also set Reminders for individual Post-it Notes.

You'll get the best results from the square 3x3- or 11x11-inch Post-it Notes in neon pink, electric blue, limeade, and electric yellow. You can buy these through the Evernote Market, but you can also find them at big box retail stores, such as Target or Walmart.

MOLESKINE NOTEBOOKS

If you're a pen-and-paper aficionado, Evernote's Moleskine notebooks might be a good fit for you. They're available through the Evernote Market (see the Notebooks category at

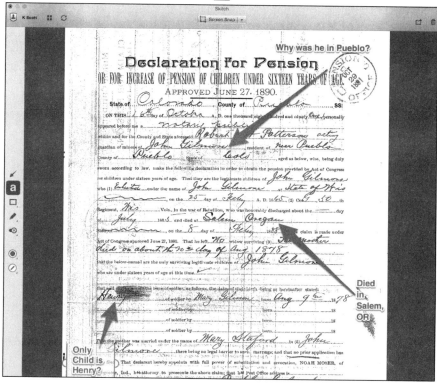

Skitch allows you to annotate a PDF even if you're not an Evernote Premium subscriber. The interface looks just like the one that Premium subscribers have in the Evernote app.

<www.evernote.com/market>) in a variety of sizes and styles, and they're branded with the Evernote logo.

These notebooks don't offer any special powers; notes in them can be photographed using the Evernote camera, but so can notes on any other sheet of paper (or whiteboard, or napkin, or any other surface). They do, however, come with some special stickers that allow you to auto-tag your notes (see images **E** and **F**) and a special pocket in the back to hold the stickers. Some of the notebooks also come with a three-month Premium subscription to Evernote, which helps offset the cost of the notebook by quite a bit.

SKITCH

The Skitch app allows you to annotate PDFs, photos, and web clippings. If you're an Evernote Basic or Plus user who wants to be able to annotate PDFs, this is a great work-around.

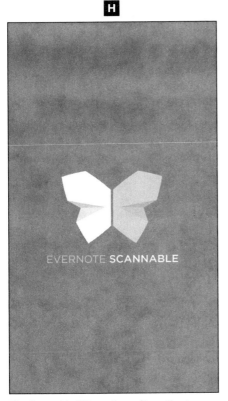

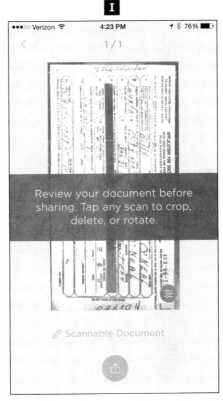

The Scannable iOS app is an alternative to manually scanning documents to send to Evernote.

Scannable auto-detects your document's margins (as in the case of this SS-5 form) and gives you many options to enhance and share the file.

You can use Skitch to add arrows, text boxes, highlighting, and other tools in the same way you'd annotate an Evernote note (image **G**). When you're done, you can save the PDF in Evernote. The interface looks just like the Evernote annotation screen (see chapter 6), so there's no learning curve.

SCANNABLE

Scannable (image **H**) is an Evernote-integrated app for iOS devices. It allows you to take photos of documents that the app automatically crops and enhances (image **I**). The Scannable app also makes it easy to share your documents via e-mail or iMessage or to add them to Evernote.

Evernote has incorporated some of the features of Scannable into its own built-in camera, but Scannable seems to do a better job of cropping and enhancing documents. Of

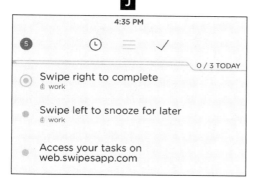

J

4:35 PM

0 / 3 TODAY

Swipe right to complete
🏢 work

Swipe left to snooze for later
🏢 work

Access your tasks on
web.swipesapp.com

Swipes acts as an enhanced task manager
for Evernote.

POWER-USER TIP

Finding New External Tools
Evernote has made partnering with other companies a priority. That means new tools are coming out all the time to make Evernote more useful. The best place to stay on top of product announcements is on the official Evernote blog **<blog.evernote.com>**.

course, there are some genealogical documents that you wouldn't want cropped, because you might miss important notes in the margins. If that's not a concern for the document you're working with, Scannable is a great alternative to manually feeding documents into a scanner. To get the app, search the Apple App Store for *Scannable*.

SWIPES

The Swipes app works on both Android and iOS devices. It integrates with Evernote to convert your notes into tasks. If Evernote's to-do list feature isn't quite robust enough for your needs, Swipes is an excellent alternative.

To use this tool, create an Evernote tag called #Swipes and assign it to notes you want to turn into tasks. They'll be pulled into the Swipes app, where you can assign priorities, edit your tasks, and use a number of other task-management tools. You can even hit the snooze button on a task (image **J**).

You can get the app by searching for *Swipes* in the Apple App Store or Google Play store.

KEYS to SUCCESS

✳ Integrate handwritten notes with Evernote using the Penultimate app, Post-it Notes, and Moleskine Evernote Smart Notebooks. These tools are helpful for situations in which you prefer to write notes by hand.

✳ Use Skitch to mark up PDFs in Evernote if you're a Basic or Plus user. This app gives you the same PDF annotation capabilities that Premium subscribers enjoy as a built-in feature. (So if you're a Premium subscriber, Skitch is redundant.)

✳ Try the Swipes and Scannable apps for enhanced project and document management capabilities. Look for other tools to enhance your Evernote experience in the Evernote App Center.

Protecting Your Evernote Files

Evernote is an extremely popular tool, with more than one hundred million users worldwide. It's the flagship product of a healthy, growing company. That said, the software landscape can change rapidly, and there are no guarantees in life. That means it's important to keep your important data safe by ensuring that they're not dependent on a single tool (even a great tool like Evernote).

We also live in a time where keeping electronic data secure is a hot issue. The beauty of Evernote is that it's portable, so you can use it on every device you own. That's exciting—until you lose your phone or your tablet is stolen. When that happens, it's scary to think about where your data might end up. Some genealogy data can be sensitive, and if you use Evernote for genealogy, you'll probably end up using it for other parts of your life, too. Thieves can't do much with your great-grandmother's obituary, but they might be able to make use of some of your other, more personal data.

This is why it's important to talk about security. This chapter will walk you through the steps you can take to protect your data from unwanted viewers but is preserved for the people you do want to pass information on to.

PASSWORDS

Your first line of defense in keeping your Evernote account safe is fairly obvious: It's your password. Here are some basic tips for choosing an appropriate password to protect your data:

- Avoid names. Genealogists are especially prone to using the names of our loved ones, past or present, as passwords. It's likely, though, that the name is associated with you somewhere on the Internet. Ever posted a public family tree? A query? An answer to a message board? If so, others can figure out the names of your family members.

Password Power

Password-management applications are fantastic for keeping all of your online accounts safe (not just your Evernote account). They allow you to create unique, random, unguessable passwords for every application and website you use.

You can set your password manager to log in to each website automatically, so you never have to remember any of those unwieldy passwords. I don't even know what my password is for my bank, my Ancestry.com account, or my Evernote account. I don't have to, because my password manager handles it for me. That frees up my aging brain cells for genealogy. Lifehacker **<www.lifehacker.com>** frequently reviews and ranks password management applications, including LastPass **<www.lastpass.com>**, Dashlane **<www. dashlane.com>**, KeePass **<www.keepass. info>**, and 1Password **<agilebits.com/ onepassword>**. Check Lifehacker for the latest recommendations.

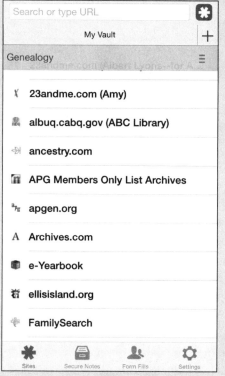

I use a tool called LastPass to generate and track unique, hard-to-guess passwords for the genealogy websites I use. I can even set them to log me in automatically, so I don't have to type in my username or password.

- Use a combination of letters, numbers, and symbols. If you can't resist the urge to use an ancestor's name as a password, at least toughen it up a bit. Smith is easy to guess, but Smith1884/1971*Iowa is tougher. You know a lot about your ancestors; use that knowledge to build tougher-to-guess passwords.
- Choose a phrase instead of a word. If you fear that you'll never remember your password if it's hard to crack, consider using a phrase to help. For example, you might start with the phrase "My grandpa James Larimore died of a rattlesnake bite in 1817." If you take the first letter of each word and substitute the tilde symbol for the rattlesnake, you get this: MgJLdoa-bi1817. That's easy for you to remember, but hard for others to guess. (This is a true story. Grandpa James was said to be such a frequent practical joker that his wife didn't believe him when he came home and said he'd been bitten by a snake. Presumably, she believed him when he died shortly afterward. I like to think that a jokester like Grandpa James might appreciate the macabre humor in using a tilde to represent the snake.)
- Create a different password for each site. We've all heard this advice, but not all of us actually apply it. A password-management application such as LastPass **<www.lastpass.com>** or KeePass **<www.keepass.info>** can make this much easier.

Two-step verification (known as two-factor authentication in most other applications) is another key weapon in the effort to keep your account safe. The basic premise of two-step verification is that it combines something you *know* (such as your password) with something you *have* (such as your cell phone). What this means: Even if someone somehow gets your password, he can't log into your account because he doesn't have your phone. Of course, if you lose your phone, this won't help much. Most compromised accounts happen thanks to offshore hackers, though, so this will protect you against the most common type of security issue. Here's how to enable two-step verification:

Applying Two-Factor Authentication All Around

Two-factor authentication is available for a variety of applications, and it's a great idea. Many banks and the social media sites Twitter and Facebook offer this; it's also an option for many major web-based e-mail services, including Gmail. It can seem cumbersome when you're setting it up, but as you become accustomed to using it, it's a great way to ensure that your important data and your Internet identity are secure. Look for this feature on the other websites you use.

1. Go to <**www.evernote.com**> and log into your Evernote account. (Note: For security reasons, you can only manage this process in the web version of Evernote, not on your computer or device).

2. Click on the Account link in the lower left corner of your screen.

3. Click on Security Summary on the left side of the screen. You'll be prompted to re-enter your password. This prevents others from changing your settings without your knowledge.

4. At the bottom of your Security Summary report, you'll see "Two-Step Verification is not enabled" (see image **A**). Under that is an Enable link. Click it.

5. You'll go through a series of prompts that will lead to a point where you'll agree to be sent a verification e-mail. Ensure your e-mail address is correct, then click the green Send Verification E-mail button.

6. When you receive the e-mail, enter the confirmation code inside it. You'll then be prompted to enter the phone number where you want to receive authentication text messages. You won't get text spam or phone calls, and your phone number won't be shared. It's used exclusively for authenticating your Evernote logins.

7. Within a minute or so, you'll receive a text message with a six-digit code (image **B**). Enter that into the Evernote screen in your web browser.

8. Next, you'll be prompted to enter a backup phone number. This is highly recommended. If you ever lose your phone, you'll be extremely glad to have the option of logging in via a code received on a backup phone. A spouse, another household member, or a friend is a good choice. If you'd rather wing it, click the Skip link (which is in tiny text on the left—you'll need a microscope to see it, but it's there).

9. You'll be shown a screen of backup codes. These are codes that you can use in case you don't have access to your phone but need to log in. Of course, you might be tempted to store these in Evernote, which is your tool for storing bits of information you might need later. But don't, because if you need them to log on, you can't access them—because you can't log on. It's best to print and store them in the same safe place you keep your Social Security card and other important, sensitive documents.

That's it. Your account is now safe. Each time you log in on a new device or from a new location, you'll be prompted to enter your password, then sent a text message. The text message will have a unique six-digit code for you to enter. You'll have to do this only once on your mobile devices, but you might have to do it repeatedly on your computer or laptop, depending on how often your IP address/location changes or how frequently you clear your browser cookies. It might sound like a hassle, but once you

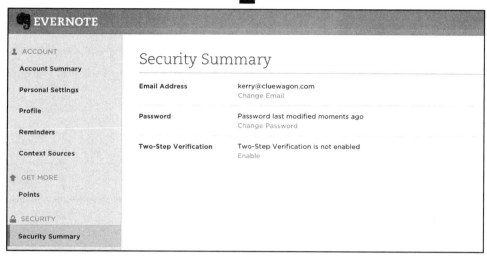

The Security Summary screen is where you'll find the option to turn on two-step verification.

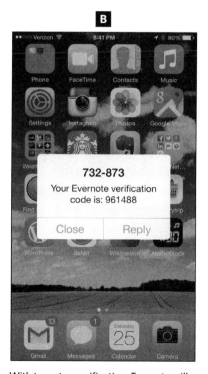

With two-step verification, Evernote will send you a text message with a special code when you log in to make sure it's really you.

get used to the process, it's well worth the effort to gain that peace of mind that comes from knowing your data are safe.

EXPORTING FILES TO PDF

If you've been doing genealogical research for a while, you can probably name a number of once-popular family tree programs that, like our ancestors, are now dead and buried. My first family tree program was the version of Family Tree Maker put out by Brøderbund. It came bundled with a program that allowed you to make greeting cards and print them on your dot matrix printer. My kids refer to this period as "the olden days."

Savvy genealogists (and savvy computer users in general, for that matter) know that it's unwise to rely too much on any one piece of software, because that software can cease to exist. The more platform-dependent your important data are, the more vulnerable you are. For that reason, it's important to convert important notes to a more ubiquitous format, such as PDF. PDFs run on their own software (the free Acrobat Reader **<get.adobe.com/reader>**), but so many of them are out in the wild that if Adobe disappeared tomorrow, someone likely would step in and fill the gap (for a price, of course). Think of it like having your home movies on VHS versus Betamax. It's easy to find companies that convert old VHS tapes to digital, because the volume of old VHS tapes means there's money to be made in offering conversion services. The same can't be said for Betamax tapes, and people who still have those are largely out of luck in terms of retrieving their movies.

As of this writing, Evernote for Windows doesn't directly convert notes to PDF, so you'll need to do this via a PDF printer (although it's likely that future versions will have this oft-requested feature). The latest version of Evernote for Mac, though, allows you to convert a note to PDF within the application. Here's how to do it:

1. Open the note you want to convert to PDF.

2. Navigate to somewhere on the note itself, then right-click (control-click on Macs). Click Convert Note to PDF from the drop-down menu that appears (image **C**).

3. In a second or two, your list of notes will include a duplicate of the one you're working on, and it will have the same name. Open it, and you'll see that it's a PDF.

4. In the top-right corner of the PDF box, you'll see three options (image **D**): The circled letter-a icon allows you to annotate the PDF (read more about this in chapter 6). The eyeball icon lets you view the PDF. The download icon lets you save the PDF to your hard drive, Dropbox **<www.dropbox.com>**, a flash drive, or a CD-R.

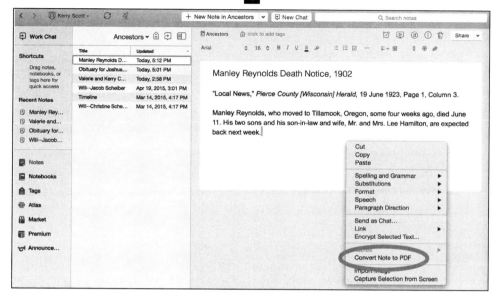

Evernote for Mac allows you to convert notes to PDF in one click.

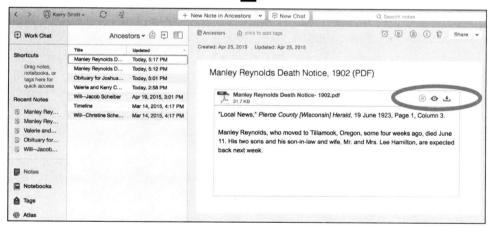

Once your note is converted to PDF, use the icons in the top-right corner of the PDF box to annotate, view, or save the PDF elsewhere on your computer.

BACKING UP ALL OF YOUR EVERNOTE DATA

It's a good idea to back up your entire collection of Evernote data from time to time. To do this, you'll need to export it, then save the resulting file to your hard drive or cloud storage (such as Dropbox). You have a few choices in terms of your file format:

- **ENEX files** can be opened only in Evernote. That's helpful if you want the option of restoring to Evernote, but it won't work if you decide to drop Evernote altogether (or if Evernote goes away). It's dependent on the Evernote platform to work.
- **HTML files** can be opened in any web browser or HTML editor. This is like saving to PDF, in that the files aren't dependent on Evernote's continued existence. If you're looking for long-term backup security, this is probably your better option.

Belt and Suspenders: My Multilayered Protection Plan

One benefit of Evernote is that it's backed up in the cloud. If your computer dies or your house catches fire, your data are safe. That's a reassuring layer of security, but it shouldn't be your only line of defense.

To protect your data completely, it's best to back it up yourself in a format that isn't platform dependent. Here's my personal backup system for my Evernote data:

- *I check to ensure everything is syncing regularly, across all devices.* This is especially important when you upgrade the operating system on a particular device or when Evernote upgrades are released.
- *I convert important notes to PDF.* I don't bother to do this with things I won't need or want in five years, such as my grocery list or my plans for the backyard overhaul. For my notes from my expensive trip to the Salt Lake Institute of Genealogy or the eighty-dollar Civil War pension file I just received, though, I want to have multiple backups.
- *I have Time Machine attached to my Mac.* This is a physical, automated backup system that resides in my office. PC users have a number of similar options in the marketplace.
- *I have a subscription to an online backup system,* Backblaze **<www.backblaze.com>**, which backs up all of my data in the cloud every day.

Using this strategy, I'm protected from most types of disaster. If my computer dies or my house bursts into flame, my stuff is backed up on both the Evernote servers and on the Backblaze servers. If Evernote vanishes tomorrow, I have my PDFs in multiple places. If hackers attack both Evernote and Backblaze, I have copies on my hard drive and my Time Machine.

Of course, if all of these things happen simultaneously, I'll probably have bigger worries than my Civil War pension files.

- **MHT files** are an option for Windows computers (but not Macs). They're a variation on HTML files, but they do a better job of preserving your note's media, such as images and external links.

Keep in mind that you can back up more than once, and in different file formats, to handle multiple types of disaster. The process of exporting your data works like this:

1. Log on to Evernote via your desktop or laptop (exporting can't be done from a mobile device or from the Web).

2. Select the notebooks you want to export by highlighting them with your mouse. If your notebooks are organized into stacks, you also can choose a stack to include all of the notes and notebooks in that stack.

3. Navigate to the top of your screen, chose the File menu, then choose Export all Notes.

4. Choose your file name, and be sure to review the location you've set to save the file so you can find it again. If you're using an online backup system such as Backblaze, make sure the end destination on your computer is a location that will be backed up in that system.

5. Choose your exported file format at the bottom of the dialog box. You'll also want to be sure to check the box next to "Include tags for each note."

6. Click Save. Double-check the location where you saved the file to be sure the file is there.

USING ENCRYPTION TO PROTECT SENSITIVE DATA

For most genealogical research, data encryption probably isn't really necessary. After all, much of what we find comes from public records, and the scandal of Grandpa Andrew's bigamy has probably faded in the past 150 years. In certain rare situations, however, you might be working on something so sensitive that it's entirely possible someone might want to access it for nefarious purposes. For example, the genealogists who research celebrities' families for the various genealogy TV shows might need to encrypt their notes. People who

POWER-USER TIP

Encrypting Your Data

Encryption is the process of converting your data into a secret code that can't be easily deciphered. The code can be translated back only via a secret password. Of course, your data are only as secure as the password you choose, so choose wisely, and make sure you'll remember it later.

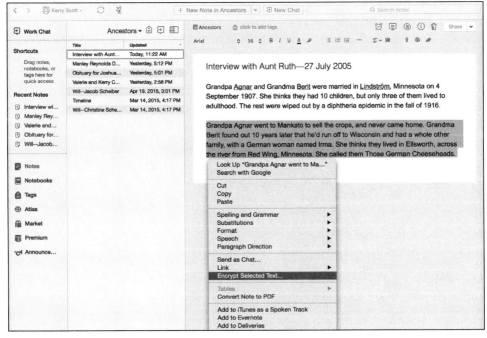

Encrypting a selection of text is quick and easy in Evernote.

Interview with Aunt Ruth—27 July 2005

Grandpa Agnar and Grandma Berit were married in Lindström, Minnesota on 4 September 1907. She thinks they had 10 children, but only three of them lived to adulthood. The rest were wiped out by a diphtheria epidemic in the fall of 1916.

•••••••• ▼

The series of dots with the drop-down arrow beside them shows you that there's encrypted text in this note.

work on paternity cases involving prominent people might also need this type of security. It's also possible that you'll enjoy Evernote so much, you'll start using it for other parts of your life. If you're storing your tax return information in Evernote, for example, you'll want to know how to encrypt it.

You can't encrypt an entire note, notebook, or stack, but you can select text and encrypt that. Here's how to do it:

1. Open the note that contains the text you want to encrypt.

2. Highlight the text you want to work with, then right-click. Choose Encrypt Selected Text from the drop-down menu (see image **E**).

3. You'll be prompted to enter a password. Choose a password you can remember, because if you forget, there's no way to recover it. Encryption means that even Evernote can't help you recover the data if you've forgotten the password. You'll also be able enter a hint in case you do forget the password, so make it a good one.

4. Click OK. Your text will disappear, and in its place will be a series of dots with a drop-down arrow (see image **F**). This is your clue that there's additional encrypted text within the note.

5. To see the text, you can click on the drop-down arrow and choose Show Encrypted Text, then enter your password. You'll also see that the option to permanently decrypt the text is located in this same menu.

KEYS to SUCCESS

✳ Choose passwords that are easy to remember but hard to guess.

✳ Consider using a password manager. These tools store your passwords securely and allow you to create unique, random, hard-to-guess passwords for each website you use.

✳ Enable two-step verification for an extra layer of security for your Evernote data.

✳ Export important notes to PDF so they can be backed up separately. This also ensures that your data will be accessible even if Evernote is no longer in business.

✳ Back up your entire Evernote collection periodically.

✳ Consider encrypting any especially sensitive notes. Be sure to store your encryption password in a secure place, because there's no way to recover it if you lose it.

EVERNOTE DATA PROTECTION CHECKLIST

☐ Begin by setting a strong password for your Evernote account. If your current password is weak, change it.

☐ Apply two-step verification to your Evernote account.

☐ Back up your Evernote data in multiple formats:

☐ PDF: Saving all your important notes in this format ensures you could access them if Evernote was suddenly no longer available.

☐ HTML or MHT: Export your entire Evernote file to one (or both) of these formats to create an additional backup.

☐ Save your Evernote backups to a location that's covered by your automatic backup service/schedule, or be sure to include the files when you back up your computer manually.

☐ Double-check that your backup files are actually ending up where they're supposed to, especially after updating your software or operating system.

☐ Encrypt highly sensitive data within your Evernote notes following the instructions in this chapter. Choose an easy-to-remember password, because there's no way to retrieve a password if it's forgotten.

☐ Store a hard copy of your encryption password in a secure location, such as a safety deposit box, to protect against memory failure.

Troubleshooting

Although Evernote is exceptionally simple to use, it's inevitable that sooner or later you'll have a question or run into an issue. Evernote's own customer support is pretty good, but you'll find a wealth of other resources available to help you troubleshoot issues. In fact, there are even places on the Internet where you can get Evernote help that is specific to the unique needs of genealogists.

E-MAIL, PASSWORD, AND ACCOUNT ISSUES

Perhaps the most common questions related to Evernote involve managing your e-mail address, password, and account status. Luckily, these issues are usually easy to resolve.

Changing Your E-mail Address

Keeping your e-mail address current with Evernote is important. You'll need it to log in, to open support tickets, and to receive password resets and other key information. Here's how to change your e-mail address:

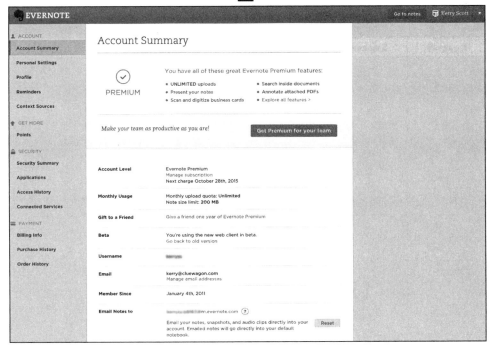

Initiate the process of changing your e-mail on the Account Summary screen.

1. Log in to your account through the web version of Evernote by navigating to **<www. evernote.com>**.

2. In the top left corner, click on Account.

3. A pop-up menu will appear. Click Settings.

4. You'll see a page called Account Summary (image **A**). In the middle, you'll see your e-mail address listed. Click the link beneath it called Manage e-mail addresses.

POWER-USER TIP

Avoid the Spam Trap

Some spam filters are pickier than others. If you find that you're missing important Evernote notifications, messages, or sharing invitations from cousins and colleagues, there's an easy solution. Go to your e-mail provider's security settings to ensure e-mails from Evernote will never be labeled spam (some providers refer to this as "whitelisting"). That way, you can be sure you'll never miss important updates or new information on a shared ancestor.

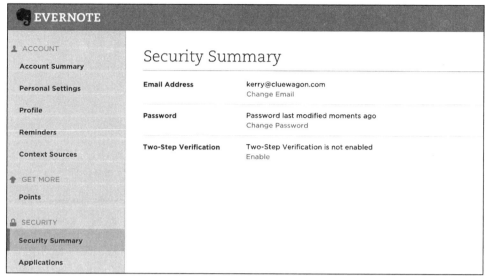

The Change E-mail link is on the Security Summary screen.

5. You'll see a page called Security Summary (image). The first option will be Change E-mail. Click that link.

6. Enter your password (so Evernote can be sure this is actually you), then enter the new e-mail address you'd like to use. You'll receive a confirmation e-mail within a minute or two. If you don't get it, check your spam filter.

7. Click the link in the confirmation e-mail, and your e-mail address change will be saved.

Changing Your Password

Computer security experts advise that it's always a good idea to change your password periodically. Some websites make that process painfully difficult, but in Evernote, it's easy. To change your password, follow these steps:

1. Log in to your account through the web version of Evernote.

2. In the top left corner, click on Account.

3. A pop-up menu will appear. Click Settings.

4. You'll see a page called Account Summary. On the left, click Security Summary.

5. Click Change Password.

6. Enter your old password, then your new one (you'll be asked to enter it twice, to avoid accidental typos). Click update.

Recovering a Lost Password

With as many online accounts as most people have, forgotten passwords are a common obstacle. If you can't remember your Evernote password, don't panic. Here's what to do:

1. Go to the web version of Evernote.

2. Click the Login link, then click Forgot Password? (image **C**).

3. Check your e-mail (be sure it's the account you used to register with Evernote). Within a minute or two, you should have an e-mail from Evernote with a password reset link. If you can't find it, check your spam filter.

Changing Your Billing Status

If you're an Evernote Plus or Premium subscriber, you'll probably need to make changes to your billing information at some point. If you're an Evernote Basic user, there's a good chance you'll want to upgrade in the future. To change your credit card number or billing method or to switch from monthly to yearly billing (or vice versa), do this:

1. Log in to your account through the web version of Evernote.

2. In the top left corner, click on Account.

3. A pop-up menu will appear. Click Settings.

4. You'll see a page called Account Summary. On the left near the bottom of the menu, click on Billing Info. From here, you can change your address, your credit card/Pay-Pal information, and your billing frequency (image **D**). Note that billing changes will take effect at the end of your current billing cycle.

TROUBLESHOOTING SYNCING ISSUES

Syncing is awesome—most of the time. Once in a while, though, you'll run into problems. If you notice that your notes aren't syncing properly, try these steps:

- Click the Sync button. It's at the top of the screen on your device, your desktop, and your web browser. If your automatic syncing isn't working, this is the quickest and easiest fix.

- Reboot your computer or device. This tried-and-true advice solves a multitude of problems.

C

The password reset link is at the bottom of the Evernote login dialog box.

D

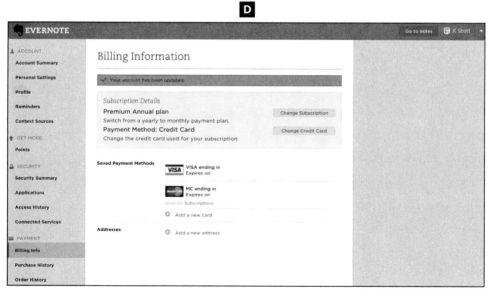

Change your payment preferences on the Billing Information screen.

- Make sure you have a good Internet connection. If you're at home, reboot your router by unplugging it for thirty seconds, then plugging it back in (it'll take a few minutes to come back online—be patient). If you're using a public Wi-Fi or cellular signal, move around a bit to see if you can get a stronger connection. If you've recently added a lot of bandwidth-heavy photos or audio clips, realize that some public Wi-Fi connections just aren't robust enough to handle syncing that much data at once. Your syncing issue will likely improve when you get home, where you're (hopefully) not sharing your bandwidth with a crowd.

- Check for updates. Are you using the latest version of Evernote that your computer or device can run? The older your version, the more likely you are to experience syncing issues.

Add a Profile Photo

You can personalize your Evernote experience a bit by adding a profile photo. This is an especially nice feature to use when you begin collaborating with cousins you haven't met in person, since people tend to respond more warmly to a real human face. To upload a photo, go to your Account Summary, then click on Profile.

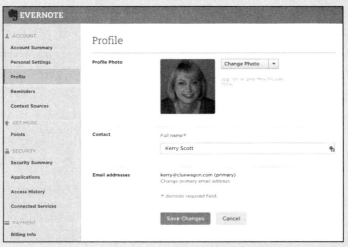

Upload a profile photo to personalize your experience and ensure your collaborators see a friendly face.

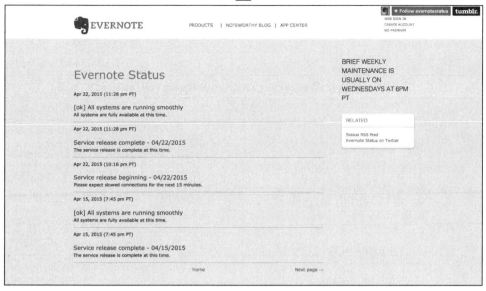

The Evernote Status page lets you see at a glance if there are system issues that might slow you down or otherwise affect your Evernote experience.

- Clean out your Trash notebook. If you have too much data or one of your trashed notes has become corrupt, clearing the Trash will resolve your sync issue.

- Check in with Evernote. It's not common, but once in a while, even mighty Evernote has connection issues. You can see for yourself what's going on by checking **<status. evernote.com>** (image).

- Go nuclear. If nothing else works, try deleting and reinstalling Evernote. Because your data are in the cloud, they will reappear as soon as you log back in. Before you do this, you should save any unsynced notes using the techniques outlined in chapter 11.

OTHER COMMON ISSUES

Although everyone is different, issues that arise while using Evernote tend to follow some common themes. Is yours on this list?

Help! I Did Something Dumb! How Do I Undo It?

On a PC, click Control-Z to undo your last action. On a Mac, click Command-Z. If you're on an iPhone or iPad, shake the device itself (gently!) to undo. As of this writing, Android, Windows, and BlackBerry devices don't yet have an Undo function.

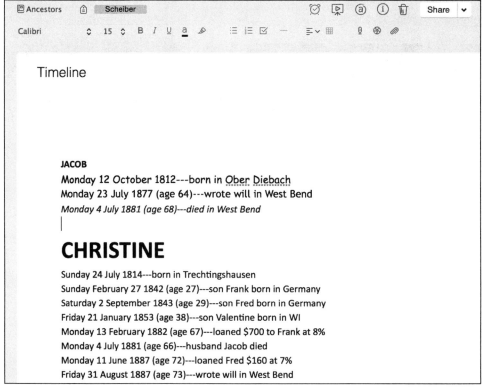

Wonky fonts in your notes can be frustrating, but they do happen (especially if you copy and paste text from other programs). You can fix them by selecting all of the text, then choosing one font and size to standardize the entire selection.

My Fonts Are a Mess—Big in Some Places and Small in Others. What Do I Do?

Highlight all of the text using your mouse (click Control-A on a PC or Command-A on a Mac). At the top of your note, you'll see a toolbar with the font choice, font size, and formatting options (image). Choose one font and one size, and all of your text will be adjusted to match your selection.

Why Isn't My Search Finding XYZ Item? I Know It's There.

It's likely that your search feature has been restricted. Next to the search box, you'll see a little magnifying glass. There's a tiny drop-down arrow next to it. Click it, and you'll see the option to narrow or broaden your search. Click Search All Notes, then try again. You can read much more about searching techniques and tricks in chapter 4.

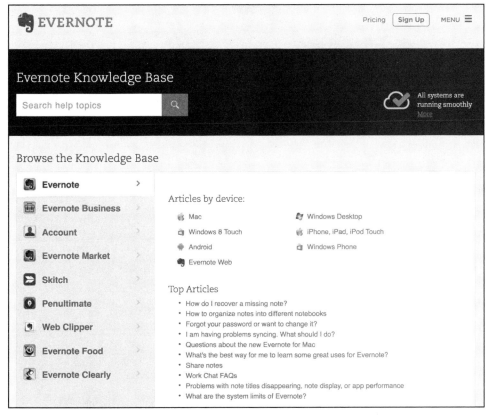

An article explaining how to resolve your issue might already be posted in the Evernote Knowledge Base.

My Note Is Missing! Where Is It?

It's probably in the Trash notebook. When you find it, look for the Restore Note button in the top left corner. Click that, and your note will return to its original home.

FINDING MORE HELP

When you've exhausted all of the routine solutions, or you have a problem that seems unusual or complicated, it's time to call in the big guns. With Evernote, there are lots of big guns. Here are your options for getting more help:

- Evernote Knowledge Base <www.evernote.com/contact/support/kb>: This is ground zero for getting help. You can search for article by device, by platform, and by a variety of other criteria (image). It's the first place to go when you're stuck.

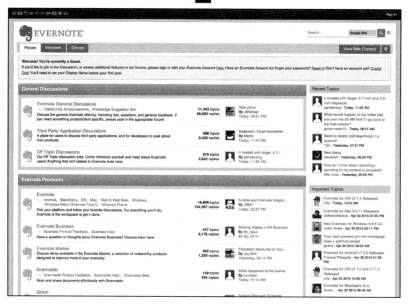

Pick other people's brains in the Evernote User Forum.

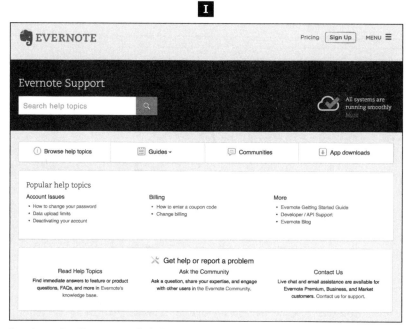

Premium subscribers can get help from a live person via the Evernote Support page.

- Evernote User Forum **<www.discussion.evernote.com>**: The forum is a great place to talk to other users about Evernote itself and add-on items such as Skitch and Penultimate (image **H**).

- Evernote Support **<www.evernote.com/contact/support>**: If you're a Premium subscriber, you can get help from a real live Evernote employee (see the Contact Us link on image **I**). There's a live chat option, or you can submit a support ticket via e-mail. I've always received a response within twenty-four hours (not counting weekends, when the Evernote offices are closed).

RESOURCES FOR LEARNING MORE

Like everything else in the technology world, Evernote changes often. New tools are released, and talking to other users is the best way to learn more about how to make the most of them. Genealogists have some unique needs with regard to Evernote, so it's especially nice when we can find help that speaks to those needs. Here are some great places to discover how others are using Evernote:

- Evernote's blog **<www.blog.evernote.com/>** and YouTube channel **<www.youtube.com/user/EvernoteVideos>**: Both of these are run by Evernote, and they have excellent tips and tricks, plus examples from real-life users. The videos are professional quality and have closed captioning available for hearing-impaired users (image **J**).

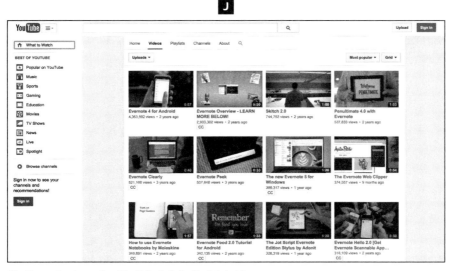

The Evernote channel on YouTube is full of helpful videos.

- Evernote Genealogists Facebook group <www.facebook.com/groups/evernotegenealogists>: This friendly group has thousands of members, and more are joining every day. If you want to bounce ideas around, ask a question, or see how others are using Evernote to solve genealogical problems, it's an excellent resource.

- Genealogy Gems <www.genealogygems.com>: Lisa Louise Cooke's podcast and website have a wealth of tips and tricks, offered in a user-friendly format.

- Moultrie Creek Gazette <www.moultriecreek.us/gazette>: Denise Barrett Olson bills her blog as "tech support for the family historian." It's full of next-level ideas for getting the most out of Evernote and a variety of other tools.

- Family Tree University <www.familytreeuniversity.com>: This sister site of *Family Tree Magazine* offers online courses to help you learn Evernote step-by-step, with instructors available to answer your questions.

KEYS to SUCCESS

✳ When you have a problem with Evernote, check the website. You'll find a variety of tools to help you resolve your issue.

✳ Network with other genealogists who use Evernote to get the most out of your experience. There's no substitute for talking to people who have the same needs and challenges you do, and it's a nice way to make new genealogy friends.

✳ Be patient, and look for ways to expand your use of this tool as you expand your search for your ancestors. Becoming an Evernote power user is a marathon, not a sprint.

✳ Consider using Evernote for other parts of your life—not just genealogy. That will allow you to become more familiar with it faster. It'll also keep your life organized so you have more time for working on family history research.

Evernote Quick Reference Guide

Using Evernote can make you a more efficient genealogist—but first you have to become efficient at using Evernote. This cheat sheet is designed to help you accomplish tasks faster by putting need-to-know information in a quick-reference format. You can download a letter-size PDF of this guide from **<ftu.familytreemagazine.com/how-to-use-evernote-for-genealogy>** to store in your research binder, next to your desktop computer—or to capture directly into Evernote.

EVERNOTE BASICS

Item	Function	How to Create	Tips
note	your primary tool for storing data in Evernote; it can contain text, photos, PDFs, web clippings, and even audio	Click the New Note button.	You can mix as many different types of data as you want into the same note. The maximum note size is determined by your membership level.
notebook	in genealogy lingo, the "parent" of notes; collect related notes on the same subject or theme into a notebook	Click the Notebooks link, then hit the New Notebooks button.	Make notebooks for research projects, activities, and/or family lines. Create a notebook called INBOX for all incoming items you haven't yet sorted or acted on.
stack	the "parent" of notebooks or "grandparent" of stacks; combine related notebooks together in a stack	From the Notebooks view, drag one notebook on top of another.	Stacks are not available on BlackBerry and Windows Phone. You can't share stacks, only individual notes and notebooks.
tag	a label you create to make related items easier to find	In the Notes view, click Click to add tags and type.	Don't go crazy creating a zillion tags; too many will become overwhelming rather than effective. Do use tags to analyze your genealogical data and spot clues you might otherwise miss.

MAXIMUM NOTE SIZE

Subscription Level	Note Size	Monthly Upload Allowance	Number of Notes	Number of Notebooks
Basic	25MB	60MB	100,000	250
Plus	50MB	1GB	100,000	250
Premium	200MB	10GB	100,000	250

E-MAILING NOTES INTO EVERNOTE

Use the commands listed here individually or together to tell Evernote how to handle the e-mails you send it.

Symbol	Function	Example
@	Place in the e-mail subject line to direct an e-mail to a specific notebook.	*@Genealogy* sends to your note-book titled *Genealogy*
#	Place in the e-mail subject line to add a tag to the note.	*#Smith* tags your note with the surname Smith.
!Reminder	Place in the e-mail subject line to establish a reminder; use *!year/month/day* to specify the reminder date.	*!Reminder !2017/02/28* sets up a reminder for February 28, 2017.

ANNOTATION TOOLS

Tool	Icon	Function
arrow		draws an arrow to call attention to something
blurring		blurs out a section of an image
color selector		changes the color of arrows, text boxes, and the highlighter
cropping		removes unwanted parts of an image
highlight		marks items of importance in color, like a virtual highlighter marker
rectangle		draws a box around a section of the image or document
stamp		adds a sort of "sticky note" with an icon and text on top of an item
text	a	inserts a box you can type text into
thickness selector		controls the thickness of lines and arrows

KEYBOARD SHORTCUTS

Most of the common shortcuts that work in other applications also work in Evernote, such as Control-X for cut, Control-V for paste, and Control-Q for quit (substituting Command for Control on a Mac). Find a complete list of shortcuts for Windows at **<www.evernote. com/contact/support/kb/#!/article/23168552>** and for Mac at **<www.evernote.com/ contact/support/kb/#!/article/23168732>**.

Application Shortcuts

Windows	Mac	Function
Win-A	press Caps Lock twice quickly	clip selection
Control-Alt-F or F6	Command-Option-F	search
Control-N	Command-N	create a new note
Control-Shift-N	Command-Shift-N	create a new notebook
Control-P	Command-P	print
Control-Shift-A	Command-R	reset search
Control-S	Command-S	save
Control-Shift-T	Command-Control-T	create a new tag
Control-F8	Command-Shift-T	toggle toolbar on or off

Note-Editing Shortcuts

Windows	Mac	Function
Control-Shift-> or Control-[	Command-+	increase text size
Control-Shift-< or Control-]	Command--	decrease text size
Control-B	Command-B	boldface text
Control-Shift-B	Command-Shift-U	format as bulleted list (or remove bulleting)
Control-D	Command-T (font) and Command-C (color)	open dialog box to change fonts and colors
Control-I	Command-I	italicize text
Control-Shift-O	Command-Shift-O	format as numbered list (or remove numbering)
Control-Shift-C	Command-Shift-T	insert to-do list checkbox
Control-U	Command-U	underline text
Control-Shift-V	Shift-Command-V	paste as plain text
Control-Z	Command-Z	undo

QUICK LINKS

- Evernote Knowledge Base **<www.evernote.com/contact/support/kb>**
- Evernote User Forum **<discussion.evernote.com>**
- Evernote Support **<www.evernote.com/contact/support>**
- Evernote blog **<blog.evernote.com>**
- Evernote genealogists on Facebook **<www.facebook.com/groups/evernotegenealogists>**
- Family Tree University online classes on Evernote **<www.familytreeuniversity.com/ courses/evernote-for-genealogy-bootcamp>**

Census Extraction Templates

I f you want to be able to create census record transcriptions in Evernote, you'll need to set up tables to hold all of the data. This appendix contains all the fields you'll need for each US census from 1790 to 1940. Be sure to set up additional templates for the state censuses you frequently use, too.

For your convenience, a word processing version of this appendix is available to download from **<ftu.familytreemagazine.com/how-to-use-evernote-for-genealogy>**. You could use these forms to transcribe census records by hand, then capture a picture of the completed form in Evernote (note, however, that your handwritten notes may not be fully searchable). You can also use the census forms put together by *Family Tree Magazine* by visiting its website **<www.familytreemagazine.com/info/censusforms>** and clicking on the desired worksheet. As with the word processing files, you can fill them out by hand, take photos of the completed forms, and upload them to Evernote.

1790 US CENSUS

Census Question	Answer
Township or community	
County	
State	
Enumerator	
Enumeration date	
Enumeration district number	
Name of head of family	
Free white males 16 years of age and upwards, including heads of families	
Free white males under 16 years of age	
Free white females, including heads of families	
All other free persons	
Slaves	

1800 US CENSUS

Census Question	Answer
Township or community	
County	
State	
Name of institution	
Name of incorporated place	
Enumeration date	
Enumerator	
Ward of city	
Supervisor's district	
Enumerator's district	
Written page number	
Printed page number	

Census Question	Answer
Name of head of family	
Free white males under 10 years of age	
Free white males 10–16 years of age	
Free white males 16-26 years of age	
Free white males 26-45 years of age	
Free white males 45 and over	
Free white females under 10 years of age	
Free white females 10–16 years of age	
Free white females 16–26 years of age	
Free white females 26–45 years of age	
Free white females 45 and over	
All other free persons except Indians not taxed	
Slaves	

1810 US CENSUS

Census Question	Answer
Township or community	
County	
State	
Name of institution	
Name of incorporated place	
Enumeration date	
Enumerator	
Ward of city	
Supervisor's district	
Enumerator's district	
Written page number	
Printed page number	

Census Question	Answer
Name of head of family	
Free white males under 10 years of age	
Free white males 10–16 years of age	
Free white males 16–26 years of age	
Free white males 26–45 years of age	
Free white males 45 and over	
Free white females under 10 years of age	
Free white females 10–16 years of age	
Free white females 16–26 years of age	
Free white females 26–45 years of age	
Free white females 45 and over	
All other free persons except Indians not taxed	
Slaves	

1820 US CENSUS

Census Question	Answer
Township or community	
County	
State	
Name of institution	
Name of incorporated place	
Enumeration date	
Enumerator	
Ward of city	
Supervisor's district	
Enumerator's district	
Written page number	
Printed page number	

Census Question	Answer
Name of head of family	
Free white males under 10 years of age	
Free white males 10-16 years of age	
Free white males 16-26 years of age	
Free white males 26-45 years of age	
Free white males 45 and over	
Free white females under 10 years of age	
Free white females 10-16 years of age	
Free white females 16-26 years of age	
Free white females 26-45 years of age	
Free white females 45 and over	
Foreigners, not naturalized	
Agriculture	
Commerce	
Manufacturing	
Free colored males	
Free colored females	
All other persons	
Slaves	

1830 US CENSUS

Census Question	Answer
Township or community	
County	
State	
Name of institution	
Name of incorporated place	
Enumeration date	

Census Question	Answer
Enumerator	
Ward of city	
Supervisor's district	
Enumerator's district	
Written page number	
Printed page number	
Name of head of family	
Free white males under 5 years of age	
Free white males 5-10 years of age	
Free white males 10-15 years of age	
Free white males 15-20 years of age	
Free white males 20-30 years of age	
Free white males 30-40 years of age	
Free white males 40-50 years of age	
Free white males 50-60 years of age	
Free white males 60-70 years of age	
Free white males 70-80 years of age	
Free white males 80-90 years of age	
Free white males 90-100 years of age	
Free white females under 5 years of age	
Free white females 5-10 years of age	
Free white females 10-15 years of age	
Free white females 15-20 years of age	
Free white females 20-30 years of age	
Free white females 30-40 years of age	
Free white females 40-50 years of age	
Free white females 50-60 years of age	
Free white females 60-70 years of age	
Free white females 70-80 years of age	

Census Question	Answer
Free white females 80–90 years of age	
Free white females 90–100 years of age	
Slaves	
Free colored people	
Deaf and dumb	
Blind	
Foreigners, not naturalized	

1840 US CENSUS

Census Question	Answer
Township or community	
County	
State	
Name of institution	
Name of incorporated place	
Enumeration date	
Enumerator	
Ward of city	
Supervisor's district	
Enumerator's district	
Written page number	
Printed page number	
Name of head of family	
Free white males under 5 years of age	
Free white males 5–10 years of age	
Free white males 10–15 years of age	
Free white males 15–20 years of age	
Free white males 20–30 years of age	

Census Question	Answer
Free white males 30–40 years of age	
Free white males 40–50 years of age	
Free white males 50–60 years of age	
Free white males 60–70 years of age	
Free white males 70–80 years of age	
Free white males 80–90 years of age	
Free white males 90–100 years of age	
Free white females under 5 years of age	
Free white females 5–10 years of age	
Free white females 10–15 years of age	
Free white females 15–20 years of age	
Free white females 20–30 years of age	
Free white females 30–40 years of age	
Free white females 40–50 years of age	
Free white females 50–60 years of age	
Free white females 60–70 years of age	
Free white females 70–80 years of age	
Free white females 80–90 years of age	
Free white females 90–100 years of age	
Slaves	
Free colored people	
Deaf and dumb	
Blind	
Foreigners, not naturalized	

1850 US CENSUS

Census Question	Person 1	Person 2	Person 3
Township or community			
County			
State			
Name of institution			
Name of incorporated place			
Enumeration date			
Enumerator			
Ward of city			
Supervisor's district			
Enumerator's district			
Written page number			
Printed page number			
Dwelling number			
Family number			
Name of every person whose usual place of abode 1 June 1850 was with this family			
Age			
Sex			
Color			
Profession, occupation, or trade of each male over 15			
Value of real estate owned			
Place of birth, naming state, territory, or county			
Married within the year			
In school within the year			
Persons over 20 unable to read and write			
Deaf and dumb, blind, insane, idiot, pauper, or convict			

1860 US CENSUS

Census Question	Person 1	Person 2	Person 3
Township or community			
County			
State			
Name of institution			
Name of incorporated place			
Enumeration date			
Enumerator			
Ward of city			
Supervisor's district			
Enumerator's district			
Written page number			
Printed page number			
Dwelling number			
Family number			
Name of every person whose usual place of abode 1 June 1860 was with this family			
Age			
Sex			
Color			
Profession, occupation, or trade of each male over 15			
Value of real estate owned			
Place of birth, naming state, territory, or county			
Married within the year			
In school within the year			
Persons over 20 unable to read and write			
Deaf and dumb, blind, insane, idiot, pauper, or convict			

1870 US CENSUS

Census Question	Person 1	Person 2	Person 3
Township or community			
County			
State			
Name of institution			
Name of incorporated place			
Enumeration date			
Enumerator			
Ward of city			
Supervisor's district			
Enumerator's district			
Written page number			
Printed page number			
Dwelling number			
Family number			
Name of every person whose usual place of abode 1 June 1870 was with this family			
Age			
Sex			
Color			
Profession, occupation, or trade of each male over 15			
Value of real estate owned			
Value of personal estate owned			
Place of birth			
Father foreign born			
Mother foreign born			

Census Question	Person 1	Person 2	Person 3
Month born in year			
Month married in year			
In school within year			
Cannot read			
Cannot write			
Deaf, blind, insane			
Males able to vote			

1880 US CENSUS

Census Question	Person 1	Person 2	Person 3
Township or community			
County			
State			
Name of institution			
Name of incorporated place			
Enumeration date			
Enumerator			
Ward of city			
Supervisor's district			
Enumerator's district			
Written page number			
Printed page number			
Dwelling number			
Family number			
Name of every person whose usual place of abode 1 June 1880 was with this family			
Color			
Sex			
Age			

Census Question	Person 1	Person 2	Person 3
Month born if during the census year			
Relationship to head of household			
Single			
Married			
Widowed/divorced			
Married during year			
Profession, trade, or occupation			
Number of months unemployed			
Currently sick or disabled			
Blind, deaf and dumb, idiotic, insane, or disabled			
Attended school this year			
Cannot read			
Cannot write			
Birthplace			
Birthplace of father			
Birthplace of mother			

1900 US CENSUS

Census Question	Person 1	Person 2	Person 3
Township or community			
County			
State			
Name of institution			
Name of incorporated place			
Enumeration date			
Enumerator			
Ward of city			
Supervisor's district			

Census Question	Person 1	Person 2	Person 3
Enumerator's district			
Written page number			
Printed page number			
Dwelling number			
Family number			
Name of every person whose usual place of abode 1 June 1900 was with this family			
Relationship to head of family			
Color			
Sex			
Month of birth			
Year of birth			
Age			
Marital status			
Number of years married			
Mother of how many children?			
Number of children living			
Place of birth			
Father's place of birth			
Mother's place of birth			
Year of immigration			
Number of years in the United States			
Naturalized citizen			
Occupation of every person 10 and older			
Number of months unemployed			
Number of months in school			
Can read			
Can write			
Can speak English			

Census Question	Person 1	Person 2	Person 3
Owned or rented			
Own free and clear or mortgaged			
Farm or house			

1910 US CENSUS

Census Question	Person 1	Person 2	Person 3
Township or community			
County			
State			
Name of institution			
Name of incorporated place			
Enumeration date			
Enumerator			
Ward of city			
Supervisor's district			
Enumerator's district			
Sheet number			
Line number			
House number			
Dwelling number			
Number of family			
Name of every person living in this family on 15 April 1910			
Relationship to head of household			
Sex			
Color or race			
Age at last birthday			
Single, married, widowed, or divorced			

Census Question	Person 1	Person 2	Person 3
Years of present marriage			
Number of children born to this mother			
Number of children still living			
Place of birth			
Father's place of birth			
Mother's place of birth			
Year immigrated to the United States			
Naturalized or alien			
Able to speak English or language spoken			
Trade or profession			
General nature of industry, business, or establishment			
Employer, employee, or self			
Out of work on 15 April 1910			
Weeks out of work in 1909			
Can speak English			
Able to read			
Able to write			
Attended school since 1 September			
Owned or rented			
Owned free or mortgaged			
Farm or house			
Number of farm schedule			
Survivor Union or Confederate Army/Navy			
Blind in both eyes			
Deaf and dumb			

1920 US CENSUS

Census Question	Person 1	Person 2	Person 3
Township or community			
County			
State			
Name of institution			
Name of incorporated place			
Enumeration date			
Enumerator			
Ward of city			
Supervisor's district			
Enumerator's district			
Sheet number			
Line number			
Street address			
House number or farm number			
Number of dwelling house			
Number of family			
Name of every person living in this family as of 1 January 1920			
Relationship to head of household			
Home owned or rented			
If owned, free or mortgaged			
Sex			
Color or race			
Age at last birthday			
Single, married, widowed, or divorced			
Year of immigration to the United States			
Naturalized or alien			
If naturalized, which year			

Census Question	Person 1	Person 2	Person 3
Attended school since 1 September			
Able to read			
Able to write			
Place of birth			
Mother tongue			
Place of birth of father			
Mother tongue of father			
Place of birth of mother			
Mother tongue of mother			
Able to speak English			
Trade or profession			
Type of business			
Employer, employee, or works for self			
Number of farm schedule			

1930 US CENSUS

Census Question	Person 1	Person 2	Person 3
Township or community			
County			
State			
Name of institution			
Name of incorporated place			
Enumeration date			
Enumerator			
Ward of city			
Supervisor's district			
Enumerator's district			
Sheet number			

Census Question	Person 1	Person 2	Person 3
Line number			
Street, avenue, road, etc.			
House number			
Dwelling number			
Number of family			
Name of every person living in this family as of 1 April 1930			
Relationship to head of household			
Home owned or rented			
Value of home, or monthly rent			
Radio set (leave blank if no radio)			
Does this family live on a farm?			
Sex			
Color or race			
Age at last birthday			
Marital condition			
Age at first marriage			
Attended school since 1 September			
Whether able to read and write			
Place of birth			
Place of birth of father			
Place of birth of mother			
Language spoken before arrival in the United States			
Year of immigration to United States			
Naturalization status			
Whether able to speak English			
Occupation, trade, or profession			
Industry or business			
Class of worker			

Census Question	Person 1	Person 2	Person 3
Whether worked last working day			
Unemployment schedule line number			
Veteran of military or navy			
Served in what war/expedition			
Number of farm schedule			

1940 US CENSUS

Census Question	Person 1	Person 2	Person 3
Township or community			
County			
State			
Name of institution			
Name of incorporated place			
Enumeration date			
Enumerator			
Ward of city			
Supervisor's district			
Enumerator's district			
Sheet number			
Line number			
Street, avenue, road, etc.			
House number			
Number of household			
Home owned or rented			
Value of home or monthly rent			
Farm (yes or no)			
Name of each person living in this family as of 1 April 1940			
Relationship to head of household			

Census Question	Person 1	Person 2	Person 3
Sex			
Color or race			
Age at last birthday			
Marital status			
Attended school since 1 March 1940			
Highest grade of school completed			
Place of birth			
Citizenship, if foreign-born			
City or town of residence on 1 April 1935			
Country of residence on 1 April 1935			
State or country of residence on 1 April 1935			
Farm (yes or no)			
Working in non-government job the week of 24 March 1940			
If not, working in government job the week of 24 March 1940?			
If unemployed, seeking work?			
If unemployed and not seeking work, did he have a job/business?			
Engaged in housework, schoolwork, unable to work, or other?			
Number of hours worked during week of 24 March 1940?			
Duration of unemployment of 30 March 1940, in weeks			
Occupation, trade, or particular			
Kind of work			
Industry or business			
Class of worker			
Number of weeks worked in 1939			
Wages or salary received			

Census Question	Person 1	Person 2	Person 3
Earned non-wage or salary income over $50			
Number of farm schedule			
Supplementary questions (asked only of people on lines 14 and 29)			
Place of birth of father			
Place of birth of mother			
Language spoken in home in earliest childhood			
Veteran?			
If child, is veteran-father dead?			
War or military service			
Social Security number issued			
Deductions for Federal Old Age Insurance or Railroad Retirement made?			
Deductions made from less than half, half, or more than half of wages?			
Usual occupation			
Usual industry			
Usual class of worker			
For women—married more than once?			
Age at first marriage			
Number of children ever born (excluding stillbirths)			

Genealogy Conference Planner

Attending a genealogy conference? Evernote is particularly handy for planning ahead of time so you can get the most out of your conference experience. Go through the conference guide to plan which sessions you want to attend, then map out your days using the planner in this section. (For your convenience, a type-able PDF version of this form is available to download from **<ftu.familytreemagazine.com/how-to-use-evernote-for-genealogy>**.) Take a photo of this form using the Evernote camera so you'll have it with you during the conference. Don't forget to save your travel itinerary and confirmation e-mails in Evernote as well.

DAY ONE

Breakfast Plan	
Morning Sessions	
Lunch Plan	
Afternoon Sessions	
Dinner/Evening Plans	
Booths to Visit	

DAY TWO

Breakfast Plan	
Morning Sessions	
Lunch Plan	
Afternoon Sessions	
Dinner/Evening Plans	
Booths to Visit	

DAY THREE

Breakfast Plan	
Morning Sessions	
Lunch Plan	
Afternoon Sessions	
Dinner/Evening Plans	
Booths to Visit	

DAY FOUR

Breakfast Plan	
Morning Sessions	
Lunch Plan	
Afternoon Sessions	
Dinner/Evening Plans	
Booths to Visit	

Research Worksheets and Templates

Whether you've been doing genealogy for twenty years or twenty minutes, you understand the need for forms and worksheets to keep your research organized. As you've learned in this book, Evernote makes all those forms even more useful by instantly indexing their contents when you import them as images or PDFs (if you're a Premium subscriber). So this book wouldn't be complete without our versions of two key research worksheets no genealogist can live without:

- a five-generation ancestor chart
- a family group sheet

You can download free letter-size PDFs of these worksheets from **<www.familytreemagazine. com/freeforms>**. In addition, this section includes templates for the research forms described in chapter 8:

- correspondence log
- research log

The best way to use the log templates is to download them in word processing format from **<ftu.familytreemagazine.com/how-to-use-evernote-for-genealogy>**. You can then copy the tables in those files and paste them directly into an Evernote note. Use that note as your template and customize however you'd like with additional rows or columns.

FIVE-GENERATION ANCESTOR CHART

Chart # ____
1 on this chart = ____ on chart # ____

see chart #

1

birth date and place

marriage date and place

death date and place

spouse

2

birth date and place

marriage date and place

death date and place

3

birth date and place

death date and place

4

birth date and place

marriage date and place

death date and place

5

birth date and place

death date and place

6

birth date and place

marriage date and place

death date and place

7

birth date and place

death date and place

8

birth date and place

marriage date and place

death date and place

9

birth date and place

death date and place

10

birth date and place

marriage date and place

death date and place

11

birth date and place

death date and place

12

birth date and place

marriage date and place

death date and place

13

birth date and place

death date and place

14

birth date and place

marriage date and place

death date and place

15

birth date and place

death date and place

16

17

18

19

20

21

22

23

24

25

26

27

28

29

30

31

FAMILY GROUP SHEET OF THE

_____ FAMILY

	Source #
Full Name of Husband	
His Father	
His Mother with Maiden Name	
Full Name of Wife	
Her Father	
Her Mother with Maiden Name	
Other Spouses	

	Source #
Birth Date and Place	
Marriage Date and Place	
Death Date and Place Burial	
Birth Date and Place	
Death Date and Place Burial	
Marriage Date and Place	

Children of This Marriage	Birth Date and Place	Death Date, Place and Burial	Marriage Date, Place and Spouse

CORRESPONDENCE LOG

Date	Via	Item	Cost	Notes

RESEARCH LOG

Date	Call Number	Description of Source	Purpose of Search	Results

INDEX

ACKNOWLEDGEMENTS

I thought writing a book would be a lonely experience. I was wrong. There were lots of people who helped make this book possible.

I probably shouldn't tell the world, but Allison Dolan has actual magic powers. I am astonished that she was able to turn what I sent her into a real book. Andrew Koch also provided valuable help and advice throughout the process.

Mary Penner provided support and encouragement from the beginning, and it made all the difference.

The members of the Albuquerque Genealogical Society warmly welcomed me to talk to them about Evernote in the early days of this book's inception. I asked them to stand in for you, the reader, and tell me what they'd need to know to move from beginner to Evernote enthusiast. They rose to the challenge, and many of the points you've read about here are thanks to their thoughtful questions and comments. Mike Blackledge deserves special recognition for his work in this regard.

Denise Barrett Olson **<MoultrieCreek.us/Gazette>** and Mark Reider **<ReiderFamily. com>** cheerfully allowed me to use material from their websites, and my cousin Valerie Peters agreed to lend me her great-grandmother for the section on Presentation Mode.

Finally, my husband Rick kept the household running and the kids fed and entertained while I hunkered down in my office for weeks. My son Charlie brought me many cans of Diet Coke, and my daughter Livy said, "You should write that book, Mom, so you'll be just like Laura Ingalls Wilder" (she's in for a bit of a letdown). The best kind of family to have is one that says, "Of course you can, and we'll help" when you want to try something. I have that, and I'm very grateful.

ABOUT THE AUTHOR

Kerry Scott is a genealogy instructor and blogger at Clue Wagon **<cluewagon.com>**, twice named one of the *40 Best Genealogy Blogs* by *Family Tree Magazine*. After fourteen years in corporate human resources, Kerry "retired" and began focusing on her genealogical research. A former online editor for *Family Tree Magazine* and Family Tree University, Kerry continues to teach for Family Tree University—including courses on Evernote. She's active in the Association of Professional Genealogists and in the online genealogical community.

ISBN: 978-1-4403-4383-4

Other Family Tree Books are available from your local bookstore and online suppliers.

For more genealogy resources, visit **<shopfamilytree.com>**.

19 18 17 16 15   5 4 3 2 1

DISTRIBUTED IN CANADA BY FRASER DIRECT

100 Armstrong Avenue

Georgetown, Ontario, Canada L7G 5S4

Tel: (905) 877-4411

DISTRIBUTED IN THE U.K. AND EUROPE BY

F&W Media International, LTD

Brunel House, Forde Close,

Newton Abbot, TQ12 4PU, UK

Tel: (+44) 1626 323200,

Fax (+44) 1626 323319

E-mail: enquiries@fwmedia.com

DISTRIBUTED IN AUSTRALIA BY CAPRICORN LINK

P.O. Box 704, Windsor, NSW 2756 Australia

Tel: (02) 4577-3555

fw

a content + ecommerce company

PUBLISHER AND COMMUNITY LEADER: Allison Dolan

EDITOR: Andrew Koch

DESIGNER: Julie Barnett

PRODUCTION COORDINATOR: Debbie Thomas

4 FREE
FAMILY TREE TEMPLATES

- decorative family tree posters
- five-generation ancestor chart
- family group sheet
- bonus relationship chart
- type and save, or print and fill out

Download at <ftu.familytreemagazine.com/free-family-tree-templates>

More Great Genealogy Resources

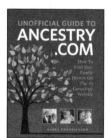

UNOFFICIAL GUIDE TO ANCESTRY.COM

By Nancy Hendrickson

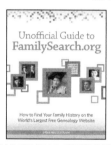

UNOFFICIAL GUIDE TO FAMILYSEARCH.ORG

By Dana McCullough

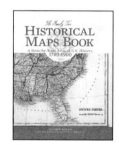

THE FAMILY TREE HISTORICAL MAPS BOOK

By Allison Dolan

Westminster Public Library
3705 W. 112ᵗʰ Avenue
Westminster, CO 80031
www.westminsterlibrary.org

sellers and **<shopfamilytree.com>**, or by calling (855) 278-0408.

<www.facebook.com/familytreemagazine>